Save the Stratford Canal!

Save the Stratford Canal!

GUY JOHNSON

DAVID & CHARLES
North Pomfret, Vermont 05053

This book is dedicated to the many organisations and individuals that have worked for and on the southern section of the Stratford-upon-Avon Canal, but particularly to Michael J. Fox and John L. E. Smith, who were key figures in making restoration possible, and to David E. Hutchings who made it happen.

British Library Cataloguing in Publication Data

Johnson, Guy
Save the Stratford Canal!
1. Stratford-upon-Avon Canal—Conservation
and restoration
I. Title
627′.136′0942489   TC664.S/

ISBN 0–7153–8424–4

Filmset in Monophoto Plantin
by Latimer Trend & Company Ltd, Plymouth
and printed in Great Britain
by Redwood Burn Ltd, Trowbridge
for David & Charles (Publishers) Limited
Brunel House   Newton Abbot   Devon

Published in the United States of America
by David & Charles Inc
North Pomfret   Vermont 05053   USA

Contents

	Preface	7
1	Seeds are Sown	9
2	The Way it Was	19
3	The British Transport Commission and the Bowes Committee	23
4	Fighting Abandonment	31
5	Progress to Triumph	38
6	The National Trust Takes Over	46
7	Real Restoration Begins	56
8	Restoration, Year One	64
9	Year Two—to Wilmcote and Beyond	78
10	Forward to Stratford	87
11	Battles of the Bancroft Basin	97
12	The Final Push	115
13	Canal Cottages	125
14	Reopening	131
15	The Trust Takes the Freehold	137
16	Full Circle	149
	Postscript	164
	Acknowledgements	165
	Index	166

Preface

'The effect of the [Stratford] Canal restoration in 1964 was electric on cruising people like us. Instead of expecting canals to get worse and worse and fewer and fewer, we suddenly saw that they might get better and better and more and more extensive. This possibility may still be in doubt, but at least the deterioration of those days was not only stopped but reversed. Whatever happens to the inland waterways system in the future, the almost miraculous revival of the southern Stratford will stand in history.' John Gagg, *5000 Miles, 3000 Locks*

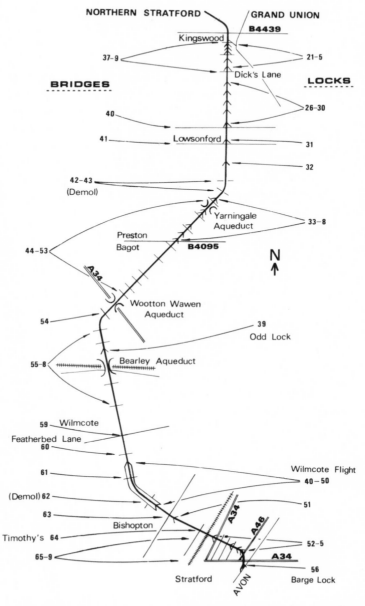

Fig 1   Diagram of the southern Stratford Canal, showing the approximate location of the salient features

I
Seeds are Sown

... if some obscure gentleman had not held a licence to navigate the canal with his canoe the Wilmcote Bridge would have been lowered—and you only have to lower one bridge to 'bitch' the whole canal. (*Sir Fordham Flower, proposing the toast 'The Stratford Canal' at the Inland Waterways Association's Festival Dinner to celebrate the reopening of the southern section of the Stratford-upon-Avon Canal, 14 July 1964*)

On Saturday 9 February 1957 a heavy Canadian-type planked canoe, loaned by the Malthouse Boatyard on the river at Stratford-upon-Avon, began what was to prove an historic voyage. It was launched from the boatyard slipway and, with two members of the committee of the Stratford-on-Avon Canal Society on board, was paddled to the steps alongside the Bancroft Gardens in Stratford, carried round the barge lock leading to the canal and launched on to the canal basin. From there, it was taken on a voyage up the canal to Hockley Heath and back, a distance of about 30 miles (48km) and 108 locks. As the locks were unusable it had to be carried round them and because of both this and the bad state of the channel, the complete return trip took six weekends, the canoe being left in various canal-side properties from one weekend to the next.

The voyage was an historic one because the standard British Transport Commission Waterways canoe toll was paid and it was the evidence of use from the toll tickets which eventually defeated the Warrant of Abandonment applied for in 1958 by Warwickshire County Council, thus making restoration of the southern Stratford Canal a possibility.

In 1957 the northern section of the Stratford Canal from King's Norton to Lapworth was in poor condition but still

9

passable by narrow boats. It was officially classified for retention for a limited period. The southern section from Lapworth to Stratford, however, was in a very sorry state. The majority of the locks were derelict, many of the pounds were overgrown by weeds and others nearly dry. The crumbling road bridge at Featherbed Lane, Wilmcote, was shored up by timbers and concrete buttresses and two of the huge baulks of timber effectively blocked the canal to anything but canoes. The last 3 miles (4.8km) or so, from Wilmcote to Stratford, were in a particularly poor condition because very little water could get past the top of the Wilmcote flight of locks, having been lost through leaks before it reached there. In Stratford itself the canal was even more neglected. A local newspaper report of the time recorded that it was only after the residents of houses bordering the canal complained of the stench from it that workmen were sent to cut down 10ft (3m) high reeds which completely choked the channel. Following the report of the Board of Survey appointed by the British Transport Commission (see Chapter 3) the southern section was classed as not justifying retention. However, the enabling acts under which all canals were built laid down a statutory obligation to maintain the navigation, and the act of 1793 authorising the Stratford Canal was no exception. Thus, parliamentary sanction was required to extinguish the right of navigation before it could be officially closed and abandoned, and this sanction had yet to be obtained.

It is believed that the last commercial boat travelled to Stratford in the 1920s and this had to be partially unloaded on the way to enable it to do so. After this, there is no evidence of any boat using the locks on the southern Stratford Canal until 1947. It has been said that a party of engineers of the Great Western Railway took a maintenance boat down the whole length of the canal and back again just before it was nationalised on 1 January 1948, but this was never proved. What is certain is that the *Quest*, 30ft (9.1m) long by 6ft

(1.8m) beam by 18in (45cm) draught, went down to Wilmcote and back at Easter 1947, during the last year of the ownership of the canal by the Great Western Railway. An account of this trip survives, by Mr E. G. Goodland of Liverpool, who took part in it.

I cannot remember definitely what kind of permit was necessary but I think we obtained it at the toll house at Kingswood [Lapworth] without difficulty.

There were three of us in the crew and we didn't have much difficulty at first, going downhill of course, but I remember difficulty with a lock at Lowsonford, as we had to take a pinion off the last lock above it in order to fit it to the gate at Lowsonford in order to make it work (assisted by the lengthsman). All the lengthsmen were assiduous in helping us as according to them no one had been through for many years—I seem to remember one saying sixteen years but this may have been an exaggeration.

Towards Wootton Wawen we encountered a deal of trouble with a thick kind of weed like felt which apparently grows on the bottom and had to do some bow hauling. But at Bearley we were using the engine again, because we overran a stop plank in the aqueduct over the railway. The two top planks were out and there was, of course, nothing to indicate the presence of the others. Fortunately we slid over without apparent damage.

We did not attempt to descend the flight of locks at Wilmcote, as we should only have had time to get down and immediately turn round and come up again, so we turned round near Wilmcote.

We had much more difficulty returning, as our progress down had caused all the gates to leak and several pounds were all but dry, and water had to be sent down from Kingswood. This was not to the liking of the lengthsmen who had, I think, kept the gates tight with ashes and turf. It was at this stage that the man who, two days before had been most enthusiastic said, in a very disgruntled manner, 'If there was many —— boats pass here I'd pack the —— job in'!

In 1946, the year before the trip by *Quest*, the Inland Waterways Association had been founded by Robert Aickman to bring together those who felt that something should be done to save the rapidly declining canals. This was the beginning of the era of enthusiasts who forced their boats through virtually unusable canals and caused officialdom to have second thoughts about closing them. In *Landscape with Canals* L. T. C. Rolt describes such a passage of the northern section of the Stratford Canal in 1947, in his narrow boat *Cressy*. The so-called 'Lifford Lane' drawbridge at King's Norton had been impassable for some time because of the substitution of a fixed deck at low level, and to enable him to get through, the bridge had to be raised by a gang of men with jacks. (The bridge is actually on Tunnel Lane but, possibly because an original error has been perpetuated, has always been referred to as Lifford Lane Bridge. Lifford Lane crosses the canal at the guillotine lock, almost at the junction.) As a result of such persistence, a protest cruise by the IWA in 1949 and even questions in parliament, the fixed deck was replaced by the present swing bridge late in 1950. Even so, boats still took up to 3 days to complete the $12\frac{1}{2}$ miles (20km) and 19 locks journey through the northern section. Some dredging was done on that section during 1951 and 1952 and traffic gradually increased. By the mid-1950s about forty boats per year were making the through passage of the northern section and about ten boats were kept on it. In 1954 some of their owners formed the Stratford Canal Club, of which more later. Weed was still a problem and a boom was fixed across the canal at Enoch's Wharf, just above the Lapworth lock flight, to prevent the locks from becoming choked by weed and to stop it getting into the Grand Union Canal.

In 1953 the Midlands Branch of the Inland Waterways Association published a report of a survey of the southern Stratford Canal in an attempt to initiate some action. One result was that the *Birmingham Weekly Post* of 29 May of that year carried a long article describing the whole canal. The lock-keeper at Lapworth was quoted as saying that only eight commercial boats passed through the northern section in 1952. Nothing further of note happened until 1956 when it became known that the County Council wanted to rebuild the road bridge at Featherbed Lane, Wilmcote, with inadequate headroom for boats, and that Stratford Borough Council were considering piping and infilling the section through that town.

In January 1956 an appeal appeared in *Bulletin* No 49 of the Inland Waterways Association, requesting local members to form a Protection Committee for the southern Stratford Canal. The inaugural meeting of that committee took place on 30 July 1956 in the Refreshment Room, Platform 6, New Street Station, Birmingham. The members were Mr P. Saunders as Chairman (he was also Chairman of the IWA Midlands Branch), Mr M. Fox as Honorary Secretary, Mr D. Burton, Mr D. Hutchings, Mrs B. Bancroft and Mr R. Marston. The principal stated aim was 'To bring about the restoration of the canal to full navigable order, from the Worcester and Birmingham Canal to the River Avon.' Subsidiary aims, the achievement of which was considered to bring the ultimate aim within closer reach, were to encourage boating and the provision of public boat trips, and to attempt to make improvements and prevent further deterioration, by the use of voluntary work parties if necessary.

Two further aims, which were not disclosed to any non-member of the IWA, were:

To prepare and maintain a survey report on the canal showing the liabilities which have fallen on to a prospective owner as a result of the actions and inaction of previous owners.

To create and train a skeleton management team to operate the canal if it is eventually found impossible to bring about its restoration except by acquiring it, or any part of it, from its previous owners.

These were ambitious aims, proposed by six people.

Letters from the Protection Committee to the press caught the attention of others and in particular the members of the Stratford Canal Club, the boating club based on the northern section. On 17 November 1956 a meeting of all interested parties was held at the Wharf Inn, Hockley Heath, on the northern section. Thirteen persons attended and decided to combine the Protection Committee and the Canal Club into a single new body, the Stratford-on-Avon Canal Society. By the end of 1956 it had a paid-up membership of eleven.

At this point, it is worth resolving the confusion which occurs over the names Stratford-*on*-Avon and Stratford-*upon*-Avon. The town and its Borough Corporation (more generally called the Borough Council) use the term 'upon' whereas the Stratford District Council calls itself 'on'. Although Ordnance Survey maps name the canal as 'Stratford-on-Avon Canal' the seal of the company that built it states it to be 'The Company of the Proprietors of the Stratford-upon-Avon Canal', and thus the canal is so named in this book. However, when the Canal Society was first formed, it apparently decided to follow the Ordnance Survey and it was not until many years later that it changed its name to the present one of 'Stratford-upon-Avon Canal Society'.

The committee members of the new Stratford-on-Avon Canal Society were well aware of the state of the southern section of the canal and one of their first decisions was to try to navigate it. The then Secretary, Michael Fox, wrote some years later in the society's magazine *Cut and Trust* as follows:

None of us had then heard of the Railway and Canal Traffic Act of 1888 [which defined the conditions under which the right of navigation of a canal could be extinguished and the canal closed]. But the Inland Waterways Association's Bulletins had frequently referred to canals being closed as a result of lack of use. We thought the canal would probably be safer for being used once in a while. We knew that all the locks were in a bad way and that the last three miles of canal were either dry or overgrown. However, above Lock 40 it seemed that a canoe would have quite a reasonable passage and we set about trying to borrow one.

Some members of the committee were in favour of trying to get official sanction for the proposed trip in the form of an official canoe licence, at the [then] standard rate of 2d per mile [1.6km] without the use of locks. As no one thought we had much chance of obtaining a licence, it was argued that it would be better to make the trip without any such formality and offer to pay if challenged. In spite of this not unreasonable argument, the formal approach was decided upon.

Obtaining the licence did not, after all, prove to be as difficult as we had expected. After a telephone call and a personal visit, the local office of British Transport Waterways agreed to issue it, from Stratford to Earlswood, although in the end the canoe was only taken to Hockley Heath. We had to assure them that we were aware of the difficulties and that we were prepared to 'take the canal as we found it'. A second licence was issued later for the return journey.

So as already noted, on Saturday 9 February 1957 the Chairman and Secretary of the Stratford-on-Avon Canal Society, John Pinder and Michael Fox respectively, set out on their historic voyage. As expected, there was a difficult stretch from Stratford to the top of Wilmcote Flight, but from there the trip was not abnormal for a canoe, except for a great deal of both floating and submerged debris. However, the canoe was a very heavy one designed for rough use on a river and was not affected. They were twice asked to show their licence, once at Lock 54 in Stratford, almost as soon as they had started, and again at Lock 21 at Lapworth, at the far end of the southern section.

From a letter received after the reopening in 1964, it transpires that this was not the only canoe ticket issued that year. A Mr Hawkes wrote of himself and a friend setting out from Wootton Wawen to canoe to Stratford some time between July and September 1957. On the Wilmcote Flight they 'met a man in a city suit' who challenged them to produce a ticket which they did not have. 'He issued us with a ticket on the spot. It was, I think, valid for one week and cost about two shillings and sixpence.' From subsequent inquiries Mr Hawkes concluded that the ticket had been issued by the Section Inspector, Frank Smith. However, the ticket was not kept and by 1964 Mr Hawkes was unable to trace any evidence of its issue, even at the British Transport Waterways office.

The next significant activity was early in 1957 when the

Canal Society wrote to the local office of BTW with the following comments and proposals:

> We cannot escape the conclusion that the [Transport] Commission regards the southern section as a liability and is unwilling to accept any more responsibility for it than is absolutely necessary.
>
> Our suggestions are based on the assumption that the Commission will not be prepared to invest heavily in its future. We do, however, ask for your co-operation in our efforts to develop those uses which are still possible without any expensive repairs. We have in mind the use of canoes, rowing boats and any other craft that can be carried round the locks. We are convinced that this section has very great possibilities for the use of pleasure craft of all kinds and that it would rival the Llangollen Canal in this respect if it were in good order.

The letter continued with an offer from the society to undertake certain tasks of clearing and maintenance on a voluntary basis. These included the removal of driftwood, rubbish and other obstructions, and assistance in reducing the leakage between Preston Bagot and Wilmcote, which was reducing the last few miles to stagnation in summer. To this end, it was suggested that the society should prepare a report setting out what it thought might be done and the extent to which it could assist.

The reply was non-committal. It implied that much would have to be done to make the canal usable even for craft not requiring the use of locks and noted that the future of the southern section might depend on the government inquiry at the time. The commission did offer, however, to accept a report from the society and subsequently to discuss the matter with society representatives.

The society's offer of voluntary work received useful coverage in the local press. This attracted the attention of further potential members who attended the first general meeting of the society at the Wharf Inn on 30 March 1957. About thirty persons were present and paid-up membership increased to over twenty, including that of the present author.

The report to BTW was sent on 9 May 1957. It was intentionally confined to the risk of flooding caused by blockage of spillways by reeds; leakage in top gates which rendered spillways ineffective by passing flood water straight down the canal; and spillways which had to be manually operated by the removal of boards. The society thought that it might obtain more response from BTW on the subject of flooding, which incurred a public liability. The report proposed the clearance of weed from spillways, patching of at least two of the leaking top gates, modification of at least one boarded spillway and the building up of low portions of the bank. It was suggested that all these tasks could be undertaken by the society, though the loan of certain items of equipment by the commission and the provision of some materials would be appreciated. The reply, not received until 15 August, and then only after inquiry, withheld permission for any voluntary work until after the report of the Government Committee of Inquiry became known.

A further early activity of the society was to organise a boat rally at Whitsun 1957 at Hockley Heath, where it had cleared a small basin behind the Wharf Inn. Only two cabin boats and some canoes were there all the time, although four more boats came and went during the weekend. A film show in September, also at Hockley Heath, attracted forty-five adults and some children to a showing of *Inland Waterways* and *Painted Boats*. A few others had been drawn into the scene, but hardly as many as had been hoped for in a hall holding 200. By the end of 1957, paid-up membership was still only twenty-eight.

I must admit that at the time I thought it was hopeless, and so, I suspect, did others in the society. Yes, we were making a gesture; we would go down fighting. But what hope was there of twenty-eight people beating a town council, a county council and a nationalised transport commission, and then to go on and restore the canal? Even to some of the enthusiasts it seemed mere day-dreams and the general populace thought their aspirations the ideas of eccentrics. Fortunately, there were a dedicated few who apparently did not see it this way and continued to work and scheme.

In these more enlightened days it may be surprising that the whole situation appeared so hopeless, except perhaps to the few visionaries. To understand it better, the general canal background of the period should be studied.

2
The Way it Was

Commercial vessels must be given priority at all times. (*Statement in early editions of British Transport Waterways' pleasure boating guides*)

Commercial traffic may have died by the 1930s on the southern Stratford Canal, but it had not yet done so everywhere. The following is a near-verbatim extract from the log of a pleasure trip in *Kingfisher*, hired from the Canal Cruising Company in Stone, Staffordshire (the second hire firm to have started up on the canals, in 1948).

Tuesday June 26th., 1956. Reached Wardle Lock Junction with Trent & Mersey canal at Middlewich at about 2.30pm., intending to turn left to Anderton. Immediately found ourselves in a rush of narrow boats. Had to hold back at junction to let a northbound BTW maintenance boat precede us down the locks and then at the third lock met a loaded pair coming up. Had to go down the lock between their motor and butty as they came up ("working turns"). Cleared lock just in time to get out of the way of four more loaded pairs going up (southbound). Found a space among the many working boats at Middlewich and moored up for shopping. After doing so, saw several more pairs going south. Eventually restarted about 4.15, following a northbound pair down the wide lock. Met six more pairs and a BTW tug between there and Anderton, which was reached about 7.0pm. in heavy rain. Seven pairs tied up there, of which six were loaded. After taking photos in very bad light, winded and returned about one mile [1.6km] south, meeting a trio! Tied up for night about 8.15.

However, Middlewich was an exception for the period. Commercial traffic was dying or dead on most parts of the canal system and pleasure traffic had barely started. On other parts of that trip, the canals were almost deserted. The log records only two boats seen moving on the Staffordshire and Worcestershire Canal between Great Haywood and Auther-ley and they were sister boats from the same hire firm. The Shropshire Union Canal was recorded as 'quite busy' with several pairs of loaded working boats including *Ibis*, *Lapwing* and *Acacia*, together with at least eight or ten other hire boats. Hurleston Locks were in very poor condition and difficult to work. The 2 mile (3.2km) pound above them was virtually dry after a long stoppage at Grindley Brook for routine maintenance (this was in mid-June—and there was no easy way then of finding out about stoppages in advance). The boat and party on it had to spend the night stranded in mid-channel part way up the pound. An entire afternoon was spent in the middle of Pontcysyllte Aqueduct, watching a cricket match down below, without seeing another boat. Imagine doing that now.

We have already noted that by the mid-1950s the northern section of the Stratford Canal had been 'improved', but it was still full of shoals, the new swing bridge at King's Norton was kept permanently locked and in summer there was duckweed up to 1ft (30cm) thick for miles above Lapworth Locks. When the author brought his first boat through the northern section early in 1957, a workman from the factory by the swing bridge cut the chain that secured the bridge with bolt cutters; the alternative was to fetch the key from Tardebigge, some 10 miles (16km) away. At the Lapworth end, having fought through the duckweed, there was the trauma of moving the weed boom, a telegraph pole or something similar secured right across the canal. Since the canal side was too shallow to get the boat in, although it only drew about 8in (20cm), opening the weed boom usually entailed a muddy paddle. Because Lapworth Locks were only used by the forty or so boats that made the through passage each year, they were in very poor condition for operating, with gates leaking and sticking and paddles either very stiff or jammed solid.

The state of the northern Stratford Canal was by no means

unique. The summit of the Leicester section was almost impassable in summer with, at best, a channel just wide enough for a boat between banks of reeds on either side or, at worst, mile after mile where this narrow channel was itself blocked by floating weed. In the summer of 1957 it took two of us $1\frac{1}{2}$ days of hard labour, much of it bow hauling, to take a small light boat the 20 (lock-free) miles (32km) from the top of Watford Locks to the top of Foxton Locks. When we arrived, the second lock down was drained and maintenance work was in progress. We were the only boat known to be moving in the area and we had been given up on the assumption that we had turned back. Unannounced, unscheduled stoppages were quite normal on the non-commercial routes (which many of them were by then) as there was a fair chance that no boat would appear. Gates that did not open or shut, or leaked torrents anyway, paddles that did not work, and all the other things at which we are horrified nowadays, were then all common occurrences. While it is true that many canal structures have seen further deterioration since, in terms of navigability of the channel by pleasure boats, the situation has vastly improved.

Working boats still existed on some parts of the system—for instance, on the northern end of the Trent and Mersey, as we have seen, and on the London to Midlands run. It was obvious, however, that their declining numbers each year indicated that their days were numbered. On the other hand, pleasure boats on canals hardly existed and their appearance on many parts of the system was a matter for comment, frequently unfavourable from some BTW staff. By going through locks we were breaking the mud and ash seals that they had carefully built up to stem the leaks in the gates—seals which, but for us, might well have remained intact the whole year round. To many of them, pleasure boats were just a nuisance. Some did their best, by any means at their disposal, to discourage pleasure boating (though others welcomed any traffic to relieve the boredom).

There were just a few pioneering hire firms, most with no more than a handful of boats each. Because the few boatyards that existed were concerned solely with working boats, a pleasure boat was very much on its own and every trip was an adventure. If one broke down it might be days, even in midsummer, before another boat came along. There were no mass-produced purpose-built pleasure boats. If it was not possible to buy or afford the cost of running an ex-working boat, any suitable boat would be used, from a converted ex-army bridge pontoon to a ship's lifeboat. Only a few hundred pleasure boats existed and most of them were of the latter types, including some of the hire boats.

The fact that the narrow canals were sinking into oblivion suited many people since it caused least trouble. There seemed little prospect of ultimate salvation for most of these canals and development was considered out of the question. Public opinion was apathetic or even hostile, with some demanding that the canals should be filled in. The few enthusiasts were considered dangerous cranks and it seemed beyond most people's understanding that any respectable person could genuinely care for a stinking half-dry ditch.

It was against this background that the Stratford-on-Avon Canal Society was trying to awaken interest in a canal that was already derelict. Even if it was reopened, what conceivably could be the use of it?

3
The British Transport Commission and the Bowes Committee

The historical background which led to the state of affairs described in the previous chapter is dealt with comprehensively in *British Canals* by Charles Hadfield. For the present purpose, it is sufficient to give a summary, much of which is taken from Hadfield, of events pertinent to the story of the Stratford Canal over the decade following nationalisation.

The Transport Act of 1947 had the primary aim of nationalising the railways but, more or less incidentally, it also nationalised thirty canals then owned by railway companies together with seventeen other independent waterway undertakings. These were combined with two waterways which were already state-owned to form, in 1948, The Docks and Inland Waterways Executive of The British Transport Commission—a body chaired by Sir Reginald Hill, formerly of the Ministry of Transport.

The Docks and Inland Waterways Executive took over about 2,200 miles (3,540km) of inland waterways of which about 1,400–1,800 miles (2,250–2,900km) were navigable (it depended on your standards). They operated 130 barges (wide boats), 650 compartment boats and 400 narrow boats, the latter mainly between London and Birmingham and the Mersey and Birmingham. In the early 1950s, 12 million tons per annum were carried on the inland waterways, about half of this being coal.

The statutory duty of the British Transport Commission was to provide efficient modern transport and its first priority on the waterways was to overtake arrears of maintenance, insofar as that was appropriate to a transport function. As Charles Hadfield notes, 'there was, of course, hardly any pleasure boating on the waterways and such as there was, the executive considered an oddity in a basically transport situation'. Nevertheless, in 1949, the executive's magazine *Lock and Quay* carried a note to the effect that it was anxious to encourage pleasure cruising, particularly if it helped to swell revenue. It was 'seeing what can be done without undue expense' to improve those waterways which 'require attention to make them serviceable' for pleasure boating. The southern Stratford Canal had, of course, already reached a state where the expense was presumably considered 'undue'.

As already noted, the Inland Waterways Association was formed in 1946 and from then onwards a number of books on canals began to appear, which led to some increase in public awareness of the inland waterways. In 1950 the Lower Avon Navigation Trust came into being, with the objective of restoring the near-derelict privately owned portion of the Warwickshire Avon from Evesham to Tewkesbury. This body began to show what volunteers could accomplish.

A new government brought in the Transport Act of 1953 which, in the course of reducing the amount of nationalisation in the transport industry, replaced the Docks and Inland Waterways Executive by a Board of Management under a weakened Transport Commission. Because there was, by now, an annual deficit of over £80,000 on the Docks and Inland Waterways Executive system, in 1954 the Transport Commission appointed a Board of Survey, chaired by a member of the commission. Its remit was to report on 'Whether all possible steps are being taken to ensure that the maximum economic advantage is being derived' and to advise on 'steps to be taken in regard to such inland waterways as can no longer be put to economic *commercial* use' (author's italics—they obviously did not think much of the pleasure potential). With such terms of reference it is not surprising that the report of this Board of Survey, published in 1955, proposed a vicious hatchet job. Some 336 miles (540km) carrying substantial commercial traffic were to be improved and developed; 994 miles (1,599km) were 'worth retaining' and efforts were to be made to encourage commercial traffic on them. However, where this encouragement failed, the canal concerned was to be added to the third group, which was '771 miles [1,240km] disused or carrying so little traffic as not to justify retention'. Of this latter, 180 miles (289km) were already closed to navigation. Waterways in this third group were, if possible, to be transferred to the drainage authorities with no navigation rights. So, after the 1955 report, more than 1,000 miles (1,609km) of waterway were under threat, being the whole of the third group plus an unknown proportion of the second group. The northern section of the Stratford Canal was placed in the second group and the southern section in the third.

Mathematical pedants may note that the total mileages of inland waterways in different parts of this chapter do not always correspond exactly. Every report of the time gave slightly different totals according to viewpoints on 'navigability', 'derelict', or even what constituted an inland waterway.

In the same year in which the above report was published (1955), the inland waterways undertakings of the British Transport Commission were separated administratively from the docks, though a few of the latter remained with their associated waterways. The inland waterways were now to be run by a sub-commission known as British Transport Waterways, with Sir Reginald Kerr as General Manager. His energetic approach to the problems on commerical waterways is only relevant here in that his remit was still transport; within that remit he was not justified in spending more on non-commercial canals than was absolutely necessary to ensure public safety. There is no denying that most of the narrow canals in general and the southern Stratford in particular were not contributing to commercial transport.

Nevertheless, according to Charles Hadfield, Sir Reginald Kerr not only saw that pleasure cruising should be encouraged on canals but he had a personal interest in doing so. In 1956 he started a small fleet of BTW hire cruisers at Chester and welcomed other private firms which were starting up. In the same year he initiated the first of a series of *Inland Cruising Guides* for pleasure boaters; No 1 was entitled *The Llangollen Canal*. The series became very popular and they are now collectors' items; the quotation at the head of Chapter 2 is from one of them. In 1957 he started 'Heart of England' passenger-carrying cruises on the Oxford Canal and although on this run the passengers spent the nights in hotels, in later cruises the boat was also used for overnight accommodation, thus becoming an 'hotel boat'. Sir Reginald was also a member of the Lower Avon Trust.

Thus, it is reasonable to suppose that Charles Hadfield is right in stating, in a personal communication with the author, that Sir Reginald Kerr had no personal wish to abandon any canal which had the slightest hope of a future. However, because his remit, as Manager of BTW, was transport and, officially, he had no money to do anything not connected with transport, he was bound by the recommendations of the Transport Commission's Board of Survey.

However, the report of that board had caused considerable controversy: the waterways enthusiasts, led by the Inland Waterways Association, claimed that the recommendations were completely biased by the Transport Commission's desire to rid itself of all the narrow canals. As a result, the government appointed an independent committee of inquiry in 1956 to 'consider and report on the country's system of inland waterways'. This committee became known as the Bowes Committee after the name of its chairman. The Bowes Committee was instructed to consider the waterways in the context of national benefit and not just as a transport system. It received evidence from eighty-five bodies, but it is, perhaps, a sign of the times that only four of these were organisations of waterways enthusiasts—namely the IWA, the Kennet and Avon Canal Association (it became a trust later), the Oxford Canal Association and the Stratford-on-Avon Canal Society. Few other such societies or associations existed in those days.

By the time the Stratford-on-Avon Canal Society realised the importance of the Bowes Committee, the nominal closing date for submission of evidence was already past. However, Robert Aickman of the IWA was able to arrange for further evidence to be accepted. Thus, during the spring and early summer of 1957 the society's Honorary Secretary, Michael Fox, was busy carrying out a survey of the Stratford Canal and preparing a fourteen-page report, which was finally submitted to the Bowes Committee on 11 July, quite some time after they had agreed to accept it. As can be imagined from its length, the report was very detailed, but for the present purpose it is sufficient to quote a few extracts which indicate its intent and concept.

Reference was first made to the northern section which was noted as '. . . navigable by pleasure craft but conditions not good' although the general condition of the Lapworth flight of locks was 'reasonable and had been distinctly improved during the past year'.

The southern section, on which the report had most to say, was entirely another matter.

Since nationalisation [in 1948] this section has been almost completely starved of maintenance and deterioration is taking place quite rapidly . . . the natural forces of decay are assisted by vandalism . . . breaking off balance beams and rolling them into the canal is one sport sometimes indulged in . . . A number of the smaller farm bridges are in dangerous condition . . . the larger bridges, though receiving no attention, are taking longer to fall down . . . The road bridge at Wilmcote needs rebuilding as the foundations have moved . . . The first lock leading from Kingswood junction is in working order but is kept locked. The condition of the others varies from apparently usable to very bad . . . In the majority, however, deterioration has been largely confined to the gates and the brickwork is still in fair condition. [After restoration started, this last statement was found to be incorrect.] This southern section is badly silted all along its length . . . Many of the pounds are not properly filled owing to leakage through rotting gates. Below Wilmcote some are empty except for a trickle along the bottom . . . When combined with bad silting or a lowered water level the almost stagnant water has encouraged an appalling growth of weeds. One pound is completely grown over with rushes and, until recently, conditions were nearly as bad in Stratford itself.

The report concluded by outlining the plans of the Stratford-on-Avon Canal Society.

On the northern section our activities will take the form of publicity for the facilities which exist and of negotiations to improve them . . . The successes of the Lower Avon Trust have created interest in voluntary restoration. There are, however, obvious objections to raising public subscriptions to restore a canal which is nationalised property. [Note here the rejection of a system later accepted by the Kennet and Avon Trust.] We should prefer to see this canal restored and developed by a national body . . . Nevertheless, as an alternative to abandonment, there is an overwhelming case for its transfer to a local body . . . empowered to preserve the navigation right and restore the navigation. In either case voluntary labour would play a part.

The long-awaited Bowes Report was published in July 1958. It divided the waterways into substantially the same groups as before. The 380 miles (611km) which were mainly river navigations were placed in Class A and rated economically viable. A further 935 miles (1,504km), mostly narrow canals, were placed in Class B, for which 'We see no prospects that receipts will suffice to meet charges properly chargeable to revenue . . . Even a steep increase from pleasure boating and angling would make no important contribution towards the upkeep of the system.'

Bowes continued:

The 1954 Board of Survey Report put the Class B waterways on probation, leaving their future in the balance. A revival of confidence in their future existence is an indispensable condition of revival of traffic on them. They [Class B] should be put into good working order and maintained to a prescribed standard for not less than 25 years.

Good working order was defined as 'restored to the widths and depths which will enable the largest craft built for use on them to navigate safely with full payloads'. Bowes was clearly thinking of commercial transport, not just pleasure boats.

The northern section of the Stratford Canal was included in Class B; the southern section, however, was relegated to Class C, a group containing 850 miles (1,368km) of waterways which were uneconomic for transport and which were to be looked at case by case with a view to 'redevelopment' or 'elimination'.

Redevelopment was not quite what might be supposed, being defined as 'kept in being as a water channel to serve primarily purposes other than commercial navigation'. However, the report did require the BTC to retain the status quo on such waterways until their case had been reviewed. For the purpose of such review the report recommended a Waterways Redevelopment Board which would need new powers to achieve ready elimination. In the past, said the report, elimination had proved too difficult by the existing legal processes. As we shall see, it was these existing laws that enabled the southern Stratford Canal to be saved. In accordance with the recommendation of the Bowes Committee, the Transport Act of 1968 extinguished rights of navigation on all nationalised waterways.

The Bowes Report did provide some slight hope for the southern Stratford Canal in that under 'redevelopment' it mentioned the possibility of transfer to other bodies such as 'Drainage Authorities, Local Authorities or, exceptionally, *Trusts*' (author's italics). Here was a straw to be seized and we shall see that it was.

In considering all the matters connected with the Bowes Committee together in one chapter, including its report which was not published until July 1958, we have moved ahead of other events that were occurring in parallel. To learn of these, we must recommence the account from the early part of 1958.

4
Fighting Abandonment

What seemed like the death knell of the southern Stratford Canal came in February 1958 when Warwickshire County Council announced that it proposed to apply to the Minister of Transport for a warrant to abandon it. In due course their intention was supported by the Corporation of the Borough of Stratford-upon-Avon. Such a warrant could be granted under the Railway and Canal Traffic Act of 1888 and provided a means of extinguishing the right of navigation on a canal. Section 45 of the act states:

Unnecessary canals. Derelict canals.
. . . and after the granting of the warrant and the due publication as required by the Board of Trade of a notice of the granting thereof, the Board of Trade may make an order releasing the canal company or other proprietors of the unnecessary or derelict canal from all liability to maintain the same canal and from all statutory and other obligations in respect thereof, or of or in consequence on the abandonment thereof.

The fight was now for the very existence of the canal. If the warrant was granted, bridges could be dropped, the channel filled in, locks ripped out, portions sold off—all without further reference to anyone.

Some of the enthusiasts' propaganda must have been taking effect since the Borough Council's support for abandonment was not without dissenters. Alderman Knight asked if the council members had any idea what it would cost to culvert the canal through the town, since if this was not done before infilling the town would be flooded. He estimated the cost at £250,000 and asked if the ratepayers were prepared to find that sum. However, the debate was won by those who saw the possibility of using the site of the canal for other purposes. The matter of the expense of infilling was, however, taken up again by further councillors at later meetings, and also by the press. The majority of councillors continued to support the view, expressed by several of them, that the canal 'had been a nuisance for years', that it was 'no longer a canal because there was no water flowing into it' and that it was 'an eyesore and a blot' on the town.

The Inland Waterways Association, the Stratford-on-Avon Canal Society and the Coventry Canal Society busied themselves in gaining support in every possible area of influence. (The Coventry Canal Society had been formed in the autumn of the previous year as a result of the successful IWA national rally in that city. One of its most active and outspoken members was David Hutchings, a member of the IWA Midlands Branch Committee and the rally organiser.) It is interesting to note that Mr C. D. Barwell, leader of the Lower Avon Navigation Trust which was restoring that river from Evesham to Worcester, felt unable to assist when approached for his support. This, he said, was partly because of other commitments but also because he was not strongly in favour of saving the canal, though he was not in any way hostile to activities in that direction.

Numerous letters of protest were written to the Borough Council, the County Council and the press, by both individuals and the various waterways groups already noted. They also jointly organised a public protest meeting on 26 April in the Town Hall at Stratford. An impressive list of speakers was assembled, chiefly by the efforts of Mr Aickman of the IWA who had the contacts; the list including: Commander Sir Peter Agnew, Bart, MP, Vice-Chairman of the Conservative Party Canals Sub-Committee and Member of Parliament for South Worcestershire, an adjoining constituency; James Johnson, MP, Labour Member of Parliament for Rugby, an adjoining constituency, and well known for his interest in outdoor pursuits; Robert Aickman, Founder and Vice-President of the Inland Waterways Association; Leslie Morton, M Inst T, General Manager of the Willow Wren Canal Carrying Company Ltd; Captain L. R. Munk, Assoc INA, Chairman of the Association of Pleasure Craft Operators and of Maid Line Cruisers Ltd; Chairman of meeting: Christopher Clifford, JP, Managing Director of the Worcester Royal Porcelain Co Ltd and a council member of the Inland Waterways Association.

A publicity stunt was also organised, primarily by David Hutchings, for the day of the meeting. This involved the secret overnight placing, in the middle of the Bancroft Basin in Stratford, of a small boat carrying the placard 'Save the Stratford Canal'. It was done secretly because no one was sure of the legality or otherwise of its presence there, and it was certain that permission for it would not have been granted by the Transport Commission.

The public response to the meeting exceeded all hopes. The official capacity of the hall, which was 150, proved totally inadequate for the actual attendance which was estimated at 400. People sat on tables all round the edge of the room and it was impossible for late-comers to find even standing room. Some were accommodated in an outer room where they could hear, but not see, the speakers; others left without being able to enter the building at all. A resolution was passed calling for the IWA and the Stratford Canal Society to press for the preservation and restoration of the southern Stratford Canal, for pleasure and commerce. The sum of £1,000 was promised to start a restoration fund and it was revealed that the National Trust might be interested in the canal. On 11 April its Executive Committee had approved in principle the preservation of selected canals by the Trust, provided it involved no financial liability, and had invited the Honorary Assistant Treasurer (John L. E. Smith) to discuss the matter with the Transport Commission or other appropriate authorities.

The fate of the canal became such an issue in Stratford that the clerk of the Borough Council issued a special memorandum to the members of the council's Roads Committee, purporting to put forward the case both for and against closing the canal. In fact, it was loaded towards closure and publication of extracts from it in the local press drew further correspondence from the individuals and bodies committed to saving the canal. Further members of the Borough Council expressed their doubts about closure at later council meetings, but the majority reaffirmed the decision to support the County Council in their application for abandonment.

On 12 June 1958 Warwickshire County Council actually made the application for 'a Warrant to authorise the abandonment of the Southern Section of the Stratford on Avon Canal [*sic*] . . . on the grounds that it has for at least three years before the eleventh day of June 1958, been disused for navigation' ('grounds' were required by the enabling act under which the application was made). It supported the application with the claim that three road improvement schemes could be carried out more efficiently if the canal were abandoned. At Preston Bagot it was proposed to fill in Lock 38 and part of the canal in order to straighten out a double bend over the road bridge. At Wootton Wawen the cast-iron aqueduct over the Birmingham road was to be replaced by a pipe to enable road widening. At Wilmcote, Featherbed Lane Road Bridge was to be replaced by one at a lower level. This was the most urgent scheme because the bridge was cracking as a result of carrying traffic far in excess of the 5 tons for which it had been built.

As part of the navigation, the bridge was still the responsibility of BTW, but their duty was only to maintain it to the original standard. If the County Council wanted to provide for the heavier traffic now using it, they had to cover the major part of the cost. Two years before, they had proposed to rebuild it with inadequate headroom for navigation, but that scheme was dropped after representations by the Inland Waterways Association about the illegality of such action. Following that, but before the County Council latched on to the idea of abandonment, they had approved another scheme to rebuild to navigational requirements at a cost of £8,000. If they could achieve abandonment they proposed to pipe the canal, infill and put the road over with no bridge, at a cost of £4,000.

It should be noted that British Transport Waterways were not associated with the application for abandonment, nor did they officially express any views on the matter. In the circumstances they did not need to, since the requirement to relinquish their liability for the canal would be satisfied whether it was abandoned, or saved and taken over by a restoration body. However, according to a personal communication from Charles Hadfield, Sir Reginald Kerr had no wish to see it abandoned—he hoped that some other body would take over both it and others like it.

Another public meeting was held on 4 July and this was followed next day by a protest cruise organised by the Coventry Canal Society. A road convoy of trailable boats and canoes went from the canal basin at Coventry to Preston Bagot, where they were joined by other boats belonging to members of the Stratford Canal Society. Here they were launched and cruised to the Odd Lock just before Edstone (Bearley) Aqueduct. The lighter boats, which were mainly canoes, were carried round the lock and proceeded over the aqueduct before turning to return to Preston Bagot. Because every boat taking part had to be brought overland to the canal, they were not in vast numbers. Nevertheless, the cruise was a great success and made such an impression on the various dignitaries and officials who had been invited to take part that it was repeated in October.

July also saw the publication of the first Stratford Canal Society *Newsletter*, which carried various campaigning articles, reported the background of the struggle and explained what the fight was about. This was distributed not only to

35

members but to the general public as a means of enlisting further support.

As required by the Railway and Canal Traffic Act, public notices of the proposed abandonment duly appeared on 15 August 1958 in the local press, on boards along the canal towpath and on bridges. Under the terms of the act there was then a statutory period of twenty-eight days during which formal objections could be made. The closing date actually fixed was 15 September, by which time the objections had to be submitted to the Minister of Transport, with copies to the County Council. A public inquiry was not automatic and the society's legal advisers said that such an inquiry, which would be the last chance to state the case against closure, would be more likely if a large number of objections were put forward.

Accordingly, the society printed and distributed thousands of forms of objection, collected them after signature and copied every one for the County Council, all within the short time available. The Coventry Canal Society also prepared similar forms and circulated them among its members. A total of 6,111 valid objections were received and forwarded to the minister, with copies to the County Council. Additionally, many persons and organisations, among them the National Trust, made their own objections by letter direct to the minister.

A particular objection made by the National Trust was to the proposed abandonment before a possible transfer to the Trust had been explored. The County Council, in reply, assured the Trust that 'No steps will be taken to press the minister to hold the public enquiry before the Trust has had the opportunity to meet such parties as it wishes and to formulate a plan.'

The society's legal advisers also wrote to the minister for clarification of the reference, in the public notice, to 'navigation during the past three years'. The reply stated that if the society could offer proof of navigation during that period by, for instance, the production of toll receipts, then the minister would not be in a position to grant the application for abandonment. It will be recalled that when the committee of the Stratford Canal Society planned the canoe trip in the early part of 1957, it had done so only with the vague feeling that the canal would be a little safer for being used once in a while. Thus, it was largely good fortune, assisted perhaps by the inherent honesty of the committee, that had resulted in toll tickets for that trip being available. Now, under threat of abandonment, they might be invaluable. Obviously, neither the County Council nor the ministry knew that the society had them, but would a canoe count? In hopes that it would, along with all the objection forms, went the two potentially precious toll tickets, plus written details of five other instances of navigation which could not, however, be supported with documentary proof.

5
Progress to Triumph

The National Trust was considering not only the southern Stratford Canal but also the southern part of the Staffordshire and Worcestershire and the Kennet and Avon, which were under threat, and even the Grand Union Canal. The Trust's considerations were fostered mainly by John L. E. Smith, a director of Rolls-Royce and of Coutts Bank, who was also Honorary Assistant Treasurer of the National Trust and later Chairman of its General Purposes Committee. He had the interest of at least two others: the Earl of Crawford and Balcarres, KT, GBE, Chairman of the Trust (who had at one time lived beside the Leeds and Liverpool Canal) and Lord Bridges, the Chairman of the Fine Arts Commission and probably the most influential person in the Trust at the time.

The main difficulties were that the Trust was unwilling to assume any financial responsibility for the canal and also that it was not prepared to be involved in controversy, especially with local government. A further factor was that the Trust was only prepared to lend its name as a figurehead; it would require strong local management to run the work. This meant that the committee of the Stratford-on-Avon Canal Society would have to be augmented by some local, well-known, professional people who were acceptable to the Trust.

Strengthening of the society's committee had also become necessary to spread the work load. For illustration, over 1,400 items of post were dispatched by the society during 1958 and the correspondence file for the first half of that year weighs over 3lb (1.3kg). Much of this load was carried by the Honorary Secretary, Michael Fox, who also had to earn his living. In a report to the committee in June 1958 he pointed out that the task ahead (which then still included most of the fight against abandonment) was quite beyond the organising capacity of the then existing committee.

Moves to obtain new, active committee members were not helped by the fact that the Inland Waterways Association, including its Midland Branch, was at that time torn by internal disagreements and in some disarray. However, at a Special General Meeting of the Stratford-on-Avon Canal Society in June 1958, Mr C. Clifford was elected as the new chairman together with four new committee members who included two solicitors. They joined four of the original members still serving. The office of treasurer was filled by co-option of the manager of the local bank at which the society had its account. The new committee immediately formed finance, legal and professional, publicity and membership, and executive sub-committees.

The new committee felt it important to have a restoration plan ready to submit to any appropriate body at any time. Accordingly, two of its members, Mr Burton and Mr Cane, made a detailed survey of the waterway and its installations and from that produced, in November 1958, a report from which a preliminary redevelopment plan was drawn up. It is clear that the committee did not, at that time, envisage a major and wholesale scheme of the kind that was eventually carried out. The 1958 plan was for piecemeal improvements on the basis of 'as and when possible', gradually extending outwards in both directions from the central section, which had remained reasonably navigable to small craft, while also encouraging use of any part of the canal that was suitable.

After the stir of the publication of the Bowes Committee Report in July 1958 and the excitement of the campaign against abandonment in the autumn, there was a lull in the obvious affairs of the canal during the winter of 1958–9. For the time being the society had done all that it could and the fate of the canal was largely in the hands of others. Everyone was waiting for the decision of the Minister of Transport as to whether or not the canal was to be abandoned. The society's *Newsletter* No 3, published in December 1958, said that the society had been advised 'not to seek overmuch publicity' until the decision was known, and that this might take some time. The newsletter also pointed out that under such circumstances the society might appear to be rather inactive, though in reality it was very busy making plans for the future. To the majority of the now 108 members, the lack of information must have made the project look moribund.

This, however, was a period during which some extremely important informal discussions took place both within the National Trust and between it, the IWA and other bodies as to what arrangements could be made for restoring and managing the southern Stratford Canal *if* it was not abandoned and *if* the Trust took it over. For instance, in September John Smith of the National Trust met with Sir Reginald Kerr of BTW and Mr Goodison, the Under-Secretary at the Ministry of Transport. He reported that they seemed keen that the Trust should have the canal. Mr Smith followed this up by taking all the important people in the National Trust, together with Mr Goodison, for a trip on the Oxford Canal 'so that they could see what each other was like' and also see what a canal could offer.

In October 1958 the National Trust decided to proceed with negotiations for the acquisition of the southern section of the Stratford Canal, subject to finance and to the approval of a satisfactory scheme for future management. The decision was not unanimous, however, and they still had many reservations. They required reports on financial aspects, on how the canal could be managed, and on what the work programme would be. They also wanted the secretary of the Trust to talk with the surveyors of the local authorities *before* bringing the canal enthusiasts further into the matter—this was because of their firm rule that the Trust should never cross local authorities if it could be avoided. The enthusiasts had been having that very effect in organising opposition to abandonment and the Trust wanted to see how strongly the local authorities felt about it.

John Smith had a further session with Sir Reginald Kerr and Mr F. G. B. Clayton, the Divisional Engineer for the South Western Division of British Transport Waterways, in whose area the Stratford Canal lay. Their view was that it would cost rather more than £100,000 to put the canal in order and perhaps slightly less than that to 'eliminate' it. Although they did not feel that the canal was worth restoring, because it had so many locks and went to a dead end at Stratford, they were prepared to co-operate if the Trust went ahead. They were in favour of the National Trust taking over selected canals as amenities and the Staffordshire and Worcestershire Canal was specifically mentioned in addition to the Stratford. Sir Reginald agreed not to make any fresh leases for the southern Stratford or to dispose of any of the canal's assets for the time being.

In February 1959 the National Trust authorised its secretary to proceed with the necessary legal formalities to enable the Transport Commission, subject to finance, to transfer selected canals to the Trust on a trial basis by way of lease determinable by the Trust after ten, or preferably, five years. The Trust's internal memoranda show that they were already thinking about 'Mr David Hutchings on a paid basis and a Committee with Mr Clifford to help run the management'. In March the Trust agreed the principle that selected canals were objects for which a public appeal by the Trust would be appropriate. In April 1959 the Trust's General Purposes Committee accepted the Finance Committee's recommendations to lease the Stratford Canal, on the basis of John Smith's financial report.

Some small-scale work had taken place on the canal during the winter of 1958–9, for in November 1958 the Canal Society had received permission from BTW to undertake general towpath clearance and tidying up at Preston Bagot. This site was chosen because it was very much in the public eye from a road which crossed at that point, and was also in bad condition. By the early part of 1959 regular work had also started at Lowsonford and in Stratford and plans were being made to start at Bishopton. At this stage, however, all the work was simply to improve towpaths.

The Stratford site was particularly important for prestige purposes as Stratfordians had complained for years about the disgusting state of the canal in the town. Saturday 28 February 1959 was a landmark, for on that date the Canal Society was permitted to start work on the water channel itself. Initially, the work on the channel was concentrated on the pound below Maidenhead Road in Stratford. The pound was drained and a start made with small parties of volunteers who came from Coventry and Birmingham, as well as locally. Mud, tin cans and weeds were dragged out, largely by hand. For two weeks the Territorial Army helped with a drag-line and winch. In order to finish the job as quickly as possible, continuous evening work was organised and carried out by a small hard-working band of local members, led by committee member Don Burton.

The result was a transformation: as *Newsletter* No 5 of June 1959 put it, 'where once there was a mass of rushes, there is now a sheet of water some 260 feet [79m] by 40ft [12m]. It was finished in haste so that it would be ready for a visit in May of the Redevelopment Committee set up as a result of the Bowes Committee Report, to consider the future of certain canals including the southern Stratford. The Redevelopment Committee was obviously impressed by what had been achieved. John Smith, who accompanied the inspection, reported unofficially that 'they were all in favour of saving the canal except for two who could not make up their minds'. He also noted that the next step was to reach agreement with British Transport Waterways and the highways authorities about the bridges. In this context, however, the secretary of the National Trust had reported during the previous October an assurance from the Ministry of Transport that 'if the canal were revived they would bear the cost of repairing Wilmcote Bridge'.

The work parties moved on to the next pound, the one above Warwick Road, and work was now extended to the channel as well as the towpath at all the other sites. At Preston Bagot, where the towpath had been cleared during the previous winter, the waterway between the road bridge and the next (accommodation) bridge was cleared by three persons who camped there over Whitsun, assisted by others on a daily basis. This was possibly the first-ever canal work camp. At Bishopton, a semi-mechanised method of clearing weeds from the channel was tried because doing so manually was slow and very hard work. A large and heavy rake-like device, several feet wide and with tines perhaps 2ft (61cm) long, was winched across the canal by a tractor, tearing out the weeds as it went. To prevent it from riding up over the dense growth of reeds it was weighted down and, as far as possible, steered. This was achieved by having some intrepid person 'ride the rake'—an exceedingly hazardous business, apt to lead to impromptu immersion in very muddy water. The rake was somewhat more efficient than hand work, but it was still painfully slow and laborious and, viewed in relation to 13 miles (21km) of canal needing attention, rather pathetic. The efforts of work parties at this time were noble, but scarcely more than a gesture. Nevertheless, they proved to be very worthwhile because they indicated to those who had the canal's fate in their hands that the enthusiasts really meant business.

On 22 May 1959 the news broke that the application by the County Council for a warrant of abandonment had failed. The letter from the Ministry of Transport said:

I am directed by the Minister of Transport and Civil Aviation to refer to your notice of objection to the application which was made to him on 11th June 1958, by the Warwickshire County Council for the grant of a Warrant and Order of Abandonment under Section 45 of the Railway and Canal Traffic Act, 1888, in respect of the Southern Section of the Stratford-upon-Avon Canal as a 'derelict' canal on the ground that it had been disused for navigation for at least three years previously.

I am to inform you that the Minister has been advised that he is not in a position to proceed with the grant of a Warrant of Abandonment because it has not been established that this section of the canal has been disused for navigation within the meaning of the said section 45 for at least three years before the date of the said application.

Thus, the southern section of the Stratford Canal was saved by two pieces of paper: the toll tickets purchased by the committee of the Stratford-on-Avon Canal Society for the canoe trip in early 1957. Unfortunately, the toll tickets were never returned from the ministry—presumably they are still there in some long-forgotten file.

The *Birmingham Post* hailed the news with the headline 'STRATFORD CANAL WILL REMAIN OPEN: SOCIETY'S TRIUMPH' and most of the local papers contained lengthy reports. The society's chairman appeared on BBC television. This amount of interest by the media has to be seen in context: this was well before inland waterways became fashionable—indeed, before most of the public were even aware that they existed. Any mention in the media was an indication of growing interest.

The County Council's Road Committee debated the matter on 10 June, one year less one day after it had decided to apply for the warrant. Now, however, there was nothing that it could do, although it considered that if the bridge at Wilmcote had to be 'rebuilt to accommodate pleasure craft' a contribution to its cost should be forthcoming from those interested in the canal's restoration. Years later, long after the canal had been restored and reopened, the author was giving a talk on canals to a local organisation. It touched on the fight against abandonment and, as usual, presented the County Council as the villains of the piece. In the question session afterwards a gentleman arose and said:

I was the County Surveyor at the time and I think some of the credit for the eventual restoration of the canal should go to the County Council—if it had not been for us applying for the warrant of abandonment you would never have mustered sufficient interest and public support to enable its restoration.

While it seems unlikely that they had any such benevolent intentions at the time, he possibly had a point. Perhaps the County Council gave it all a good push by offering itself as a Goliath for the canal enthusiasts' David to beat.

6

The National Trust Takes Over

As a result of a statement by John Smith at the Canal Society's third AGM in May 1959, a local newspaper reported that

... subject to the satisfactory outcome of present negotiations with the Ministry of Transport and British Waterways [*sic*], the National Trust has agreed to take over the southern section of the Stratford-upon-Avon Canal.

By early October, the Inland Waterways Redevelopment Advisory Committee had approved the Trust's restoration scheme and had recommended the Minister of Transport to find money towards it, as the Trust had asked. The problem of Wilmcote Bridge had been settled between British Transport Waterways and the County Council: it was to be rebuilt with proper headroom. The lease of the canal and an option to acquire it had been virtually agreed between the Trust and BTW, the only outstanding point being the supply of water.

On 17 November 1959 an agreement was signed between the National Trust and the British Transport Commission. By sheer coincidence, the date was the third anniversary of the formation of the Stratford-on-Avon Canal Society. Subject to the approval of parliament, the southern section of the Stratford Canal would be transferred to the Trust for an initial period of five years, at a peppercorn rental, after which the Trust would have the option of retaining it indefinitely. During those five years the Transport Commission would pay the Trust £1,500 per year, this being the annual amount it claimed to be losing on the section. The news received wide press coverage, including some of the national dailies.

Because Stratford Borough Council remained adamant that it did not want boats in the Bancroft Basin, the secretary of the Trust wrote in advance of the formal announcement as follows:

As you may know, agreement has now been reached with the Transport Commission. The National Trust appreciates that this matter may cause your council some uneasiness and I want to give you the following assurances. The Trust will not only prohibit boats from mooring in the Bancroft Gardens but from stopping, for even a moment. Boats will only be seen in the basin and then only for the few minutes necessary to work the lock. . . . We do not expect much difficulty [in enforcement] because we should be surprised if an absolute maximum of ten boats a day arrived at Stratford by canal and that only in the height of the season.

When the time came, this prohibition was not in fact enforced, initially because the council banned mooring in the only other possible place, the river bank which it owned, and eventually because the council's attitude softened as many of its members decided that boats were not such a nuisance after all.

The transfer to the National Trust was incorporated in the Transport Bill of 1960, which received royal assent on 29 July of that year. The formal take-over took place on 29 September 1960, more than four years after the first moves had been made to save the canal. The committee of the Stratford-on-Avon Canal Society was appointed as the Local Management Committee, responsible to the Permanent Secretary of the National Trust, Mr J. F. W. Rathbone. The committee thought that this put it in charge of the restoration but it emerges from Trust records that this was not quite what the Trust intended: it appears to have seen the Local Management Committee as an instrument for implementing decisions taken at Trust headquarters. Many of the areas of responsibility were never defined and as time went on this led to increasing disharmony between the Trust and the Local Management Committee. Thus, the moment of the Canal Society's greatest triumph was, paradoxically, also the beginning of a decline in its importance. From then onwards its committee found that it was able to exercise less and less control over the course of events, though it took some time to realise this.

On the appointment of the committee of the Canal Society as the Local Management Committee, John Smith and R. S. Latham, the Trust's agent and solicitor at Tewkesbury, were co-opted to it. David Hutchings, who was by now chairman of the IWA Midlands Branch, was appointed Canal Manager, responsible to the Trust through the chairman of the Canal Society; this of course meant that he could no longer be a voting member of the Stratford committee. Mr O. Hancox and Mr C. J. Gilbert, the two lengthsmen previously employed on the southern section by BTW, continued their duties under this new management. In order to gather new members from among the ranks of canal enthusiasts, the National Trust made an arrangement whereby members of the Stratford Canal Society could become full members of the Trust at reduced rates.

All capital expenditure on restoration was to be dealt with by the National Trust Head Office. Routine maintenance expenditure, for which it was expected that sufficient funds would be available from the estimated income of £3,500 per annum, was to be dealt with by the Local Management Committee via its own bank account. This latter 'routine' expenditure was to include payment of David Hutchings at a rate in line with that of other Trust staff of similar age, and his expenses. It was also suggested that the committee should buy a second-hand Land-Rover for Mr Hutchings, at £250 or so, out of income. The only part of the canal for which Mr Hutchings was not to be responsible was the cottages, which were to be the responsibility of Sir Dawson Bates, Regional Secretary of the National Trust.

1 Featherbed Lane Bridge, Wilmcote, shored up by baulks of timber. 1957

2 'Riding the rake'. Early clearance work at Bishopton in 1959. The person apparently sitting in the water is attempting to steer the rake as it is dragged across the canal by a cable which leads through a pulley on the opposite bank and thence back to the winch of the tractor on the towpath

3 Dredging near Lapworth, April 1961. An example of what was later realised to be inefficient dredging, because too much mud has been left in the channel. The 'mud boards' along the towpath can be seen

4 Shaping a new bottom-gate sill to fit the new gate which has already been installed. Note the small clearance between the gate and the floor of the lock chamber, which causes operating problems when rubbish builds up on the lock floor. Lock 38, Preston Bagot, September 1962

In spite of the official take-over, all-out efforts on restoration still could not start: there remained the problem of where the money was to come from. The National Trust had obtained estimates for restoration based on various assumptions:

1 Allowing for all work except clearing and hedge cutting to be done by contract at normal commercial rates for labour and materials: £51,490.
2 Allowing in addition for unskilled labour in locks to be done by volunteers: £46,490.
3 Allowing in addition for half the repuddling of leaking banks to be done by volunteers: £41,990.
4 Allowing in addition for half the dredging to be deferred or done by volunteers: £38,090.

It was thought realistic to accept assumption No 3, which produced a rounded estimate of £42,000. At the time of the take-over, the only income, as noted above, was from a few small rents and sale of water, the latter being at Stratford to the gasworks and to British Railways for steam engines. In earlier days water had also been supplied from Edstone Aqueduct to engines on the line below, but this had already ceased. This meagre income covered the wages of the three staff now employed but left little to spare.

During the dispute about abandonment, the Ministry of Transport had produced official estimates of £120,000 for abandoning the canal and £130,000 for restoring it. These figures were based on the assumption that either form of work would be done entirely by contractors. It now became possible to use the ministry's own figures to support the restoration by arguing that as a result of the National Trust taking over, neither of these costs would fall upon the ministry. It was, in effect, saving at least £120,000 based on its own estimate. The Trust had been in negotiation with the ministry on finance for some time before the take-over and had originally asked for a contribution of £35,000 towards the restoration. However, the ministry finally offered £20,000, and that only on condition that the National Trust *first* guaranteed the remaining £22,000. The ministry grant, when paid, was to be made by instalments and in arrears on receipt of certificates signed by the supervisor and countersigned on behalf of the National Trust. The work was also to be inspected regularly by a Mr Thomas from the Ministry of Transport. Each instalment of the grant was to bear the same proportion to the expenditure incurred as did the grant to the total estimate. This proviso gave rise to considerable book-keeping problems as it was not easy to allocate sections of the continuing overall expenditure to individual parts of the project which could then be certified as completed.

Until the guarantee of the Trust's £22,000 could be made, restoration could not start and the Local Management Committee was instructed to do nothing more than routine maintenance. This had already increased and indeed some steps towards restoration had commenced, as soon as it had become known that the Trust was definitely taking over. This was particularly the case in Stratford where, as has already been noted, residents had been complaining for years about the appalling state of the canal. The work parties who had started restoration in Stratford some eighteen months before the formal take-over had cleared two pounds, which was a good start but only part of what was necessary. Mr Hancox, the lengthsman who lived at the since demolished cottage by the side of Lock 54 in Stratford, was therefore asked to tackle further clearing. Starting at the Bancroft Basin and working up the canal, he pulled weeds out of the channel, cut back hedges, cleared up and burned rubbish, and so on. With the continued assistance of the volunteers led by Mr Burton, by early 1961 the canal was cleared right through the town to the gasworks on the outskirts. Further clearance had also been progressing steadily at Bishopton under the auspices of the Midlands Branch of the Inland Waterways Association, led by David Hutchings even before he became Canal Manager.

Other projects had also been started before the National Trust put the temporary ban on restoration work and some of these could not be stopped because firm orders had been placed. In any case, their cost could be covered, if necessary, from the Canal Society's own funds. The first of these was the purchase of a steam pump for £70. This was already mounted inside a steel hull which also accommodated a coal store and cabin. The steam engine drove a centrifugal pump of very large capacity, the water being drawn up through pipes over the stern and discharged amidships.

The second project that was already in hand concerned lock gates. The top gate of Lock 23 had been in a state of imminent collapse for some time and in the summer of 1960 volunteers had fitted stop planks and removed the old gate. The cost of replacement gates had worried the committee for some time since British Transport Waterways estimated £350 and £550 for top and bottom gates respectively, if made of oak to the original design. This was prohibitive if the restoration was to be done within the specified tight budget. Pre-stressed concrete or steel gates had been considered and a design for the latter, prepared by the IWA Midlands Branch, had been costed at £220 for a 'one-off' top gate, or £159 if ordered in quantity. Although BTW had been trying steel the committee had never been happy about departing so far from tradition, and indeed BTW eventually abandoned the use of steel gates. Messrs Wyckham Blackwell, a local timber firm at Hampton-in-Arden who had experience in making sluice-gates, were asked to suggest and quote for an economical design in oak. The eventual design arrived at after some consultation departed very little from the originals and the quotation was £99 for a top gate and about double that for a bottom one, made in partly-seasoned oak.

There was a good reason for the wood being only part-seasoned. Mr Butler, the Head of Wyckham Blackwell, explained to the Restoration Committee that the only way to season timber properly is to cut it up into the required sizes and then let it stand for several years. However, the sizes of timber required for lock gates were so unusual that there was little likelihood that anyone in the country would have a stock of properly seasoned oak in those sizes. Thus, the alternatives were to cut up timber into the correct sizes, stack it for several years and then make the gates—an unacceptable delay—or to use partly seasoned timber. This comprised timber in the round which had been seasoning in stock for some time but which was, of course, uncut. Timber of this nature had been supplied by the firm in large quantities to BTW for the manufacture of lock gates, so this seemed a reasonable compromise.

It was felt necessary to test the design so Mr Clifford, the society's Chairman, underwrote the purchase and installation of a new top gate for Lock 23 and this gate had been ordered before the Trust formally took over. As this was to be the society's first experience of hanging a lock gate, Mr Clayton, South Western Divisional Engineer for BTW was asked to provide professional assistance and his staff came prepared for a two-day job. In the event, during October 1960, the gate was fitted by BTW staff and volunteers within a few hours. This was the first real piece of *restoration* on the Stratford Canal.

With the benefit of many years' hindsight, there has been criticism of the durability of these cheap gates, many of which were in very poor condition after less than 20 years' use, as compared with a reasonable expected life of 30 to 35 years. However, it must be remembered that it was a matter of what was possible at the time for the price that could be afforded.

A third project which could have been affected by the temporary ban on restoration work was the reopening of the wharf at Lapworth. This continued, however, but classified as maintenance rather than restoration. The wharf lies alongside Lock 21, the first on the southern section, and had been the original repair yard for the canal. For some years the buildings there had been let to a car-component packing firm, but just before the take-over the lessee agreed to relinquish a portion. This eventually provided enough accommodation for an office, store, washroom and kitchen for the use of David Hutchings and the volunteer workers. The repair yard itself had been fenced off from the lock side. This fencing was removed and, with considerable manual effort, the ground levelled off to the edge of the lock so that heavy equipment could be loaded into boats. It had been intended to use ready-mixed concrete on this job but the expense was not permissible with money supplies not yet guaranteed; the whole job was done by hand.

Meanwhile, an appeal had been launched to raise the £22,000 required. It began with the £1,000 which had been promised at the original protest meeting in Stratford in 1958. The next landmark came at the annual dinner of the Inland Waterways Association during the winter of 1960–1 at which John Smith gave a resumé of the situation and appealed for funds. At that dinner, promises were made amounting to a further £8,000. In February 1961 the Pilgrim Trust announced that it was prepared to make £10,000 available immediately to restoration funds. This brought the guaranteed amount so close to the target figure that the National Trust was able to persuade the ministry that the whole amount would soon be raised, and the ministry made its £20,000 available.

So the real restoration now began, with a nominal starting date of 1 March 1961. It had taken five years to reach that stage.

7
Real Restoration Begins

After five years of campaigning, negotiating and planning, restoration work on the southern section of the Stratford Canal finally started in earnest on 1 March 1961. It was organised by the Committee of the Stratford-on-Avon Canal Society acting as local agents for the National Trust and managed by Mr R. D. E. (David) Hutchings who, at the age of 33, had given up his career as an architect in order to do so. By this time he was living at Lapworth on his converted narrow boat *Ftatateeta* which was moored in the first pound of the southern section, the first lock, No 21, being still usable. He later moved to the barrel-roofed cottage by No 22.

A certain amount of equipment had by now been acquired—begged, borrowed or, as a last resort, bought. The boat-mounted steam pump which had been bought for £70 had been repaired and modified by committee member John Pinder. Unfortunately, it was soon discovered to be unsuitable since it was designed to work from the lower end of a lock whereas the restoration plan required work to start from the upper end of the canal and proceed progressively downwards. Diesel pumps were therefore hired and the steam pump was eventually sold. It is believed that its hull was used as the basis of the cabin-boat *Iron Duke* after the machinery had been stripped out.

British Transport Waterways donated the 'shear-legs' (a tripod for suspending lifting gear, for use over locks) which had previously been used by them on the southern section. The Rover Company provided, at a cost of £200, a second-hand Land-Rover with a true value of around £400, the difference being seen as a donation to the restoration.

A second-hand Priestman Cub drag-line excavator was obtained from the manufacturers at the favourable price of £750 after negotiations on behalf of the National Trust by the Turriff Construction Corporation of Warwick. This firm also provided a full-time man to work the excavator at 'a rate for charity'; fitted the shear-legs with appropriate tackle; lent a diesel pump for the whole three-year period of the restoration; and supplied the services of its Chief Engineer, Mr Keer, MICE, as Honorary Adviser. A concrete mixer was lent by the Stratford firm of Lumley Saville and a tractor with hydraulic tipping gear by Massey Ferguson. A dumper was hired temporarily at £1 per day and it was agreed to purchase one as soon as possible at a cost not to exceed £175. Further purchases included £100 worth of hand tools and £22 worth of steel stakes, the purpose of which will emerge later.

Other firms co-operating, often giving equipment or supplying it at favourable prices, were John Allen & Ford Ltd of Oxford; Brown and TAWSE Ltd, Manchester; Duckhams Ltd; Racasan Ltd; Dockers Paints Ltd; Shell BP Ltd; and Mallinger Ltd of London. Additionally, negotiations were in progress with British Transport Waterways to enable the removal and re-use of paddle gear from the closed portions of the Wyrley and Essington Canal.

There was a vast amount of work to be done. BTW estimated that out of the seventy-four lock gates on the section, it was not worth considering the repair of more than ten, and even this subsequently proved to be optimistic. Each gate to be replaced would have to be lifted out, measured and individually ordered since no two were exactly the same because of different heights as well as minor variations in widths.

The walls of most of the lock chambers were bulging and in many cases would require extensive rebuilding. Some were crumbling and in imminent danger of collapse; some had collapsed. The problem was most serious on the Wilmcote Flight. Some of the movement had taken place with hardly any cracking on the surface and the brickwork often appeared sound until a bulge was removed to reveal an empty space behind. Bricks had originally been laid at right angles to the surface of the wall to tie the layers together and prevent this type of separation ('headers'), but these had split clean in half. The cost of the necessary work on lock chambers and gates had been estimated by Mr Clayton of BTW at £14,000 for materials and £6,800 for labour.

The whole 13 mile (21km) length of the canal needed dredging and it was estimated that 200,000–300,000 cu yd (150,000–230,000m³) of mud would have to be removed— and a cubic yard (0.76m³) of mud weighs well over a ton. The cost of carting all this away was prohibitive, so it was planned to dump most of it on adjacent fields if permission could be obtained or, otherwise, on the towpath. Even so, Mr Clayton estimated the cost of dredging at £7,800.

The Priestman Cub drag-line had been chosen for its very narrow track, as it would be easier to use on the towpath, but before it could even get there it would be necessary to cut most of the 13 miles (21km) of hedge, which was gigantic in places, and to trim or fell some trees. As professional hedge laying cost around £320 per mile (1.6km), it was decided that the volunteers would have to do it.

Extensive bank repairs were also required. For many years prior to the take-over, maintenance by British Transport Waterways had two main objectives: to avoid complaints of local flooding by farmers and to ensure that a continuous supply of water reached its two abstraction customers in Stratford. Since the only source of water supply to the southern section was and still is from the Lapworth end, this water had to pass right down the canal. Over the years the banks had been tunnelled by small animals such as rodents and trodden down by big ones such as cows, tree roots had penetrated and bank leaks had steadily proliferated. To prevent leakage through the banks while maintaining a flow of water, many pounds had been lowered by cutting away the crests of the weirs, or by making holes at the appropriate level in the lock gates. Once levels had been lowered, the destructive forces had attacked again at the new, lower, water line with the result that by the commencement of restoration, at least 6½ miles (10.5km) of bank were porous to much of their original depth. Before the canal could be refilled to its proper level these banks would have to be sealed. The method proposed was one which was used by BTW elsewhere, which consisted of cutting a deep narrow trench in the bank with a mechanical digger and filling this trench with a mixture of Bentonite clay and sand. Water reaching this mixture caused it to expand and partially set to form a seal. The cost of doing this where necessary was estimated by Mr Clayton at £6,500 for materials and £9,000 for labour.

All these problems are relatively commonplace for voluntary restoration groups nowadays, but in 1961 no restoration group had tackled this sort of work on such a scale before and the prospect was somewhat daunting to many, if not to David Hutchings.

The one major structure which did not seem to need immediate attention was Bearley Aqueduct. In May of 1958, the National Trust had commissioned a survey of it from Dr Cyril Boucher, MICE, and he reported:

With the possible exception of the south abutment, I see no likelihood of any expense beyond normal maintenance required for a considerable period, perhaps for the 5 to 20 years mentioned in your letter.

The following were eventually employed on the restoration: Mr D. Hutchings (Manager), Mrs Wakeling (Secretary), Mr Gilbert (lengthsman, ex-BTW), Mr Hancox (part-time lengthsman following retirement in February 1961, also ex-BTW), Mr French (drag-line driver), Mr Berry and Mr Beran (assistants to Mr Hutchings) and Mr Glover (labourer). Mr Berry had come originally as a volunteer but stayed on as an employee.

It was decided that it was essential to begin the restoration at the Lapworth end and to work down the canal, so that the canal itself could be used to transport equipment to the working site in the same way as it must have been when the canal was first built. The working plan was divided into three one-year periods. The canal was to be opened to Lock 31 at Lowsonford by March 1962 (2.1 miles (3.3km), 10 locks); to the top of the Wilmcote Flight by March 1963 (a further 7.9 miles (12.6km), 9 locks); and to the Avon at Stratford by early 1964 (the remaining 3 miles (4.8km) 17 locks).

The plan for initial work was for restoration to reach Lock 25 at Dick's Lane by the end of June 1961 and the estimated cost for doing so was:

Bottom gate (and extras) for Lock 21	£275
Bottom gate (and extras) for Lock 22	£330
Bottom gate (and extras) for Lock 23	£305
Bottom gate (and extras) for Lock 24	£305
Bottom gate (and extras) for Lock 25	£80
Contingencies	£205
Wages, excavator driver	£200
Fuel, excavator and tractor	£50
Hire of plant and pumps	£50
Total	£1,800

The first lock gate was hauled out for measuring in mid-February, the Priestman Cub drag-line, with its driver, arrived at the end of that month and the Allen digger, which was to dig the trenches for the Bentonite, was on site by the beginning of March. By the committee meeting of 29 March, David Hutchings was able to report that, 'Two more bottom gates have been removed for measuring, three lock chambers and one pound have been dredged.' Already there was 'difficulty in disposing of dredged mud' and 'delay in the delivery of lock gates . . . the first one not likely to arrive for a month'. The minutes also note that a few Bailey bridges would be needed for spanning locks, that it had proved necessary to cut hedges down to 3½ft (1.06m) in order to operate the Cub dredger, that there was good attendance at work parties and that the Boy Scouts were expected at Easter.

In April, the minutes record that the Birmingham Angling Association had agreed to pay £100 rent for their access to the towpath, instead of the £7 they had previously paid, and to make a donation of 100 guineas (£105). The rent was for access, not fishing rights, since the latter were the property of the riparian owners and not of the canal owner, that is, the National Trust. By the next month, however, these negotiations had been broken off because it had emerged that the BAA wanted long-term security of tenure in exchange, which the Restoration Committee was not prepared to grant.

Also in April it was noted that major repairs were commencing on the brickwork at Lock 22 and that only minor repairs would be necessary on the other locks down to No 25 (Dick's Lane). Three paddles had been delivered and installed. The new bridge at Wilmcote, built by the County Council to replace the one which had triggered off the attempt at abandonment, was now finished and Mr Hancox had been tidying up there. Casual labour was now being employed for fencing and plant maintenance and the commanding officer at the relatively nearby Long Marston Army Camp hoped to be able to provide four work parties. A total of £1,900 had already been spent and it was estimated that a further £1,100 was required for work to reach Dick's Lane—considerably more than the original estimate, but excusable when it is remembered that no one had any previous experience on which to base their figures. It was also recorded that Timothy's Bridge in Stratford, an accommodation bridge, was almost falling down and children had already carried out an unscheduled demolition of one parapet.

By August, £4,338 had been spent: one-tenth of the total cost estimated for the whole canal in one-ninth of the time estimated. This was considered to be about right and even to some degree encouraging. It was also noted that the canal was 'not getting the agreed flow of water [from the northern section] . . . consideration should be given to the installation of a flow measuring weir at Lock 22'. This concern over the flow of water even though the canal was not in use was necessitated by the need to maintain supplies to the abstraction customers at Stratford who provided some welcome, albeit small, income.

By the September committee meeting it became clear that some modifications would have to be made to the working plans for restoration.

Mr Hutchings said we could put new top gates all down the canal at any time but that bottom gates would have to wait until the pound below the lock in question had been dredged. As dredging was likely to fall behind schedule, it was agreed that top gates should be fitted ahead of schedule and bank repairs done to improve the water flow.

By this time, there was so much activity that it would be impossible to record it in every detail. In any case, the committee minutes do not record the detail: the phrase 'Mr Hutchings presented his report which was discussed and adopted' occurs with increasing frequency and few of his reports have survived as documents. Furthermore, none of the day-to-day working documentation appears to have survived, having possibly been hastened in its demise by what has been referred to as 'David Hutchings' habit of using his Land-Rover as a filing cabinet'. Fortunately for the historian, the Stratford-on-Avon Canal Society's magazine *Cut and Trust* was born at that time with the intention of presenting a quarterly progress report to all members and donors. It is a mine of otherwise unrecorded information and many parts of the chapters which follow, describing restoration work, are either directly copied or paraphrased from the magazine. The first issue appeared at the end of October 1961 with a print run of 750, but in spite of good intentions there were only three in total over the three years of restoration, with a fourth at the time of reopening. This was because they were largely written and compiled by the society's Honorary Secretary, Michael Fox, who had far too much to do. Publication of the society's *Newsletter* ceased altogether during the restoration, so with only three editions of *Cut and Trust* any member not directly involved in restoration work was decidedly starved of information. This had repercussions later because when the original stalwarts needed extra help, it proved almost impossible to attract new volunteers from among those who had by then become outsiders.

8

Restoration, Year One

An example of the condition of some of the locks before restoration is provided by Lock 27, between Dick's Lane and Lowsonford. Trees were growing in profusion from the lock walls, water was pouring through the top gate and the balance arm of that gate had rotted and been broken off. The bottom gate had long since fallen over and was lodged at an angle, the base being in the normal position but with the upper part wedged against the side of the lock. This bottom gate was one of several which had been fitted with a concrete balance beam by the Great Western Railway; the beam was resting on the ground and possibly helping to prevent the gate from falling over completely. When the gate was removed it was found to house a wasps' nest—an additional and more unusual hazard for the volunteers. The water going over the by-pass weir was supposed to flow down a brick-lined channel to the other end of the lock, but half-way down this channel the brickwork had crumbled away and the water was running out of the channel, down the bank and along the bottom of an adjoining field. It did eventually find its way back into the canal, but in the course of doing so over a number of years had built up an extensive scour.

Many lock chambers required rebuilding or repair and this was expected to be a major expense. A great deal of money was saved by the discovery that volunteers could do almost all the work, with the exception of laying the face brickwork. The technique was worked out in Lock 22, the second one down and the first to undergo major repairs, which involved both walls, from bottom to top and almost from end to end. First, the old brickwork was cut away, generally to a thickness of at least two courses of brick, then holes were made into the backing brickwork so exposed and steel reinforcements concreted in. Meanwhile, the bricks which had been removed were cleaned and stacked ready for re-use. Next, a brick wall which would form the new face wall of the lock was built at an appropriate distance from the remaining backing brickwork. The lower part of this new wall, which would eventually be below water level and thus not visible, was of concrete poured behind shuttering. Above what would become the water level the wall was continued upwards as a single thickness (4½in (11.5cm)) of original brick. Finally, the space between the new face wall and the old backing brickwork was filled with poured concrete, thus reuniting old and new. The concrete provided most of the strength of the finished structure but the original appearance was preserved by the outer surface layer of old bricks. Large quantities of concrete were required, which often had to be mixed by hand and carted to the pouring points in barrows and buckets, along narrow planks spanning the 12ft (3.6m) deep lock chambers.

Using this method there was a useful 'profit' in bricks. Because a single outer skin of brick, with concrete behind, replaced what was originally a foot (30cm) or so thickness of brick, many were left over, even after the damaged ones had been rejected. Even the latter were not wasted, being used for 'hard core'. Most of the bricks were the originals from the time of construction and were of good quality and, because the mortar holding them was soft, they were comparatively easy to clean up, though the job was tedious. Not only were the first nine lock chambers repaired without a single brick having to be bought, but the spares created were used for repairs to other structures, such as weir channels and culverts.

This technique for the rebuilding of lock walls was developed in response to the National Trust's guideline that the original character of the structures was to be preserved. However, the technique was necessarily abandoned on the

Wilmcote Flight, of which more later, after the discovery that far more rebuilding was required than had been anticipated and time and volunteers were running out.

As Lock 22 was the first major rebuilding job to be tackled, a complete outfit of scaffolding was hired for erection in it. Experience at this lock indicated that the scaffolding was an unnecessary expense and all subsequent lock repair work was done from suspended platforms. Timbers were laid across the lock, carrying chains which supported planked platforms, and these were moved around as the work progressed. So the volunteers had to contend not only with the dangers of partial collapse of the wall they were working on, but also with the physical difficulties of work from a non-rigid platform and the hazard of slipping off wet muddy planks into the muddy water below. It is perhaps just as well that the Health and Safety Act was not in force then.

The water level in the lock was, of course, lowered by draining the pound below, but this still left a foot (30cm) or so of water in the lock. When it was necessary to work right to the bottom, stop planks were put in and the remaining water pumped or baled out. The lock chambers also had to be cleared of accumulated mud and debris. The dredger could not remove it all and the last 50 tons or so had to be done by hand, either by bucket chains or by lifting tackle and barrows. The mud itself was black and stinking, well laced with broken glass and often above the wellington-tops of those working in it. This same job still has to be done at regular intervals as debris accumulates at a surprisingly rapid rate in the lock chambers and jams the gates. Nowadays, however, there is at least the inducement that the mud usually contains several dropped windlasses.

Jammed gates, especially bottom gates, are a particular problem of the southern section of the Stratford Canal. In most canal locks, including those of the northern section of the Stratford, the wooden sill against which the bottom of the gate fits when closed is raised by a foot or two (30–61cm)

5 The barge lock from the river into the Bancroft Basin, before restoration. Taken from below the lock, early in 1963, during the big freeze. The photographer was standing on the frozen river. Below the old footbridge which spanned the lock chamber the legs of skaters on the basin can be seen

6 The pound between Locks 54 and 55 in Stratford, 2 March 1963, during the first days of the thaw. The lock cottage has since been demolished

7 Lock 48 of the Wilmcote flight during demolition of the leaning approach wall. Summer 1963. The house in the far distance is Bishopton Spa, which also appears in plate 2

above the floor of the lock; in other words, the main part of the lock is rather deeper than the section on to which the bottom gate of the lock closes. This means that the gate does not reach all the way to the bottom of the lock and when it is swung the underside of the gate is well clear of the debris which inevitably accumulates in the lock bottom. By contrast, in the locks of the southern section of the Stratford Canal the sill is only slightly raised above the bottom of the lock and there is very little clearance between the underside of the gate and the bottom of the lock. Thus, the gate tends to sweep debris along with it as it is opened, eventually resulting in a tightly packed wedge of rubbish between the nearly open gate and the lock wall. This fault of the original construction may have resulted from an attempt to save money. To remedy it would require lowering the bottom of the locks, an expense which was quite out of the question at the time of restoration and remains so. The problem therefore has to be endured by boaters who find that their boats get stuck between the nearly open gate and the opposite lock wall; and the lock chambers have to be cleared out regularly to keep the locks usable.

As well as repairing the lock walls, it was often also necessary to repair the brickwork of the top and bottom approach walls of the lock. Additionally, the crests of many of the by-pass weirs round the locks had been lowered by BTW to keep water levels down. These weir crests and the associated weir channels also had to be repaired and it was usually necessary to clear them of undergrowth before this could be done.

Many of the weir channels ran through culverts and a number of these were blocked. In some cases the BTW method of dealing with such blockages had been to cut through from the weir channel into the lock chamber and so divert the water. The blockages had to be removed—no easy job down a long narrow tunnel—and the damage to the lock chamber repaired. The problem of blockages of weir culverts continued after restoration and has since been gradually dealt with by means of opening out the culverts so that channels are formed.

It was usually also necessary to replace the paddle starts (the wooden posts that support the actual mechanism) on the ground paddles and the underwater paddle doors were all removed and replaced. Some of the paddle gearing was very badly worn and was replaced by gearing taken from the abandoned part of the Wyrley and Essington Canal and from the Montgomeryshire Canal with BTW permission, and from the Thames and Severn Canal. The possibility that these canals also might one day be restored did not occur to anyone; at the time, many did not believe that the Stratford Canal could be. This 'imported' gear was superior in both original design and in condition to that being removed. However, some of the original gear was refurbished by the Royal Engineers and was retained for a time on Locks 24–9 inclusive and also on Locks 32 and 38. The mixture of gear necessitated the availability of two different sizes of windlass.

Large numbers of new lock gates were required and all were made by Messrs Wyckham Blackwell at the rate of about one gate every two weeks. Loading them at the maker's yard was simple enough because the appropriate tackle was available, but getting them to the locks was another matter altogether. The gates, weighing up to 4 tons each, were usually unloaded from the delivery lorry at the depot at Lapworth by a Royal Engineers' crane and placed on a tractor trailer. They were then taken down the towpath, or even across country, to the appropriate lock. Delivery across country often presented serious problems involving the bridging of ditches and the removal of hedges and trees, but it was the only way where access by the towpath was impracticable. So great were the problems of transport of gates that the possibility of taking them to the locks by helicopter was investigated, but did not prove feasible. Having arrived at the lock, they had to be unloaded again, turned on end and lowered into position in the lock. At most locks this had to be carried out by using the shear-legs and brute force, since the Royal Engineers' crane could not get to the locks. The shear-legs collapsed three times and the gates crashed down to the chamber floors.

Fitting lock gates is a highly skilled job. Each gate must make a watertight seal against the timber sill at the bottom of the gate and the cast-iron quoins at each side and must also swing freely from the closed to open position and back. The fitting of the new gates was at first done professionally by British Transport Waterways employees working in their own time or at weekends, or on release from their normal duties. After a time, volunteers learned to do the work. They started on paddle doors which, though much smaller, present a similar sealing problem; moved on to top gates which are the smaller of the two gates and thus easier; and eventually graduated to bottom gates. One volunteer, Brian Knight, became particularly skilled and together with his wife fitted many of the gates all the way down the canal. At that time, BTW did not fit gates during the winter but had summer stoppages for the purpose, but the voluntary work progressed all the year round; there was even an instance when, in a blinding snow-storm, the blade of the plane being used to fit a gate was shattered by ice in the wood. Most of the wooden sills were found to be rotten and were replaced at the same time.

Volunteers were not the only ones working on these jobs. Repairs to Lock 31, the fitting of gates to Locks 30 and 31, and the dredging of the pound between them was done by Royal Engineers from Southampton during a fortnight's camp in September 1961. This event is recorded in one of the coping stones of the towpath-side wall of Lock 31, the inscription of which reads: 'Rebuilt by 481 Port Maintenance Troop, Royal Engineers, September 1961.'

The first issue of *Cut and Trust*, dated October 1961, announced that with the exception of three bottom gates still awaited for Locks 26, 27 and 29, the gates of the first eleven locks had all been replaced or repaired. These locks were from No 21 at Lapworth to No 31 at Lowsonford. At first sight, this appears to be spectacular progress in about seven months and it was no doubt good publicity that it should appear so. However, with the objectivity of hindsight, it was not quite as good as it seemed. First, these were in general among the better preserved locks on the southern section and in fact the old top gates had been retained at Locks 21, 22 and 26, together with the old bottom gate at Lock 24. Second, the top gate at Lock 23 had already been replaced with a new one during the previous autumn as a 'test run' before restoration nominally started. Third, although the new bottom gates at Locks 25 and 28 were in position they had still to be fitted when *Cut and Trust* was published. A calculation indicates that in those first 7 months, on the first 11 locks, 12 new gates had actually been fitted (7 top and 5 bottom), with 2 further bottom gates delivered but awaiting fitting.

Even so, the fitting or refurbishing of lock gates was well ahead of schedule, having nearly achieved by October 1961 the target set for March 1962, with 23.5 per cent of the total lock-gate work done in 21.5 per cent of the time available. However, the dredging was going less well, with only 11.1 per cent achieved.

There were very few places on the canal where there was more than 2ft (61cm) depth of water and in many places the depth was virtually nil. The whole 13 miles (21km) including the lock chambers, needed dredging. It was all done from the bank, using drag-line excavators, because this was more efficient than using floating dredgers. Before any pound could be dredged a working party had to go ahead to level the towpath, reinforce weak points in it with timber piling and hardcore, cut the hedges back and down, and trim or remove trees. The value of trees in enhancing the scene was, however, fully appreciated and they were only cut when absolutely necessary. In particular, oak and ash were considered especially valuable and were often left despite being in the way.

The second-hand Priestman Cub drag-line, bought for £750 for the restoration work, started work in March 1961 from the Lapworth end of the canal and progress was rapid at first. The towpath at that end was wide, giving both free movement for the machine and plenty of room for dumping the spoil. For a short distance below Lock 22 a system was tried in which the mud was dumped into a trailer and taken away for disposal elsewhere, but this was soon abandoned as being too costly. Thus, wherever it was not possible to arrange to dump on adjoining fields, the mud had to be placed on the towpath and retained there by a wall of boards, themselves held in place by the steel stakes, the purchase of which was noted in Chapter 7. Some weeks after the mud had been dumped, when it had consolidated a little, these boards were retrieved for reuse. The volunteers doing this job had to work in a morass of mud which had dried out sufficiently to be sticky, levering out the timbers with spades and mattocks. In *Cut and Trust* No 1, David Hutchings wrote

... the difficulties encountered in moving and positioning the heavy mud-soaked timbers can hardly be imagined by those who have not carried out such work. Occasionally, heavy rain causes a [mud] burst and torrents of mud flow back into the canal from where it then has to be removed by shovels and buckets—again by volunteers [the dredger having moved on].

Under these working conditions it is no wonder that some of the steel stakes were missed and left in the towpath, some to survive there to this day. In all, it was necessary to build some 3 miles (4.8km) of these wooden retaining walls between Lapworth and Lowsonford.

The necessity of putting the dredgings on the towpath in places is the reason why some parts of it are now so high above the water line. For the first few years after the restoration many lengths of towpath were rough, undulating and steeply sloping for the same reason. However, most lengths have gradually been levelled off over the years by work parties.

Returning to 1961, by 7 May the Priestman Cub had reached Dick's Lane (Lock 25), having done more than ½ mile (800m) of canal in two months. This was very satisfactory progress which beat the target of reaching Dick's Lane by the end of June. Then things began to go wrong. It had proved absolutely vital to provide a firm level platform for the machine to work from, but in spite of all efforts to do so it fell from the towpath at Dick's Lane down a small embankment. It took two days to recover, using 15 ton jacks and heavy winches. Furthermore, the drag-line driver left. (It is not recorded whether the two events were connected.) He was replaced by another who also left after a very short time. The drag-line remained at Dick's Lane for weeks and no more real progress was made until David French was employed as the driver.

Although the dredging had progressed to just below the next lock, No 26, by 18 July the troubles were not over. From here to Lowsonford great difficulties were both expected and encountered. The towpath was, and still is, narrow and embanked above a stream. The embankment becomes steadily higher and steeper while the towpath becomes even narrower. The worst point is about half-way between Locks 28 and 29 where the canal is about 8ft (2.4m) above the stream and, in the pre-restoration state, the towpath sloped away steeply towards the stream almost from the water's edge. A great deal of care and a lot of extra work was needed to operate the machine at all. At the worst point, one of its tracks was several feet off the ground, supported by a stack of timber which had to be rebuilt every time the machine was moved. The mud had to be dumped on the towpath on this stretch and to retain it there a wall of boards had to be built along both sides of the towpath otherwise the mud would have flowed back into the canal on one side or into the stream on the other. Because the towpath was so narrow the mud-board wall had to be about twice as high as in other places in order to give sufficient capacity. The increased height of the mud pile led to extra pressure on the boards and they had to be more strongly staked. The longer steel stakes needed for this particular purpose cost 7s 6d each (37½p each if directly translated into today's coinage, but probably equivalent to several pounds each at today's relative costs).

These difficulties made the progress of dredging between May and October of 1961 painfully slow. By October, only 1.1 miles (1.76km) in total had been achieved since the beginning of restoration and a good half of that had been done in the first two months. At that rate, dredging of the whole canal would take about 7½ years. It was also noted that the cost of dredging was working out at about £900 per mile (1.6km). To speed things up it was decided that a larger machine should be used in the easier places and that this would have to be hired. The Trust's own Priestman Cub would continue to be used in the difficult places because it was smaller and more readily manoeuvrable and would be supplemented by a further hired Cub. A 10RB drag-line hired from Bowyer Plant Hire was thus started at Preston Bagot on 6 November 1961 and a Priestman Cub hired from Bomford and Wilkins started at Lowsonford on 15 January 1962. Both worked southwards, that is, down the canal towards Stratford and both were, of course, working on stretches not scheduled to be dealt with until the following year's programme. This was done in order to compensate for the delays being experienced on the stretches within the first year's programme.

With three machines working simultaneously, much hard work was needed from both the restoration staff and volunteers to keep them going, particularly in doing the necessary towpath and hedge clearing ahead of them.

On 10 March 1962 there was an official inspection of the year's work, the inspection party being presided over by Lord Chesham, Parliamentary Private Secretary in the House of Lords to the Minister of Transport. Also present were Mr Harrison of the Ministry of Transport; Mr Rathbone,

Secretary of the National Trust; and three members of the Inland Waterways Redevelopment Committee—Sir Geoffrey Lowles, Captain Munk (who was also Chairman of the Inland Waterways Association) and Mr J. L. E. Smith. After a meeting at the restoration headquarters at Lapworth the party travelled to Dick's Lane (about ½ mile (800m)) in the narrow boat *Emscote* owned by society member Mr S. Clover and then, for the remainder of the morning, inspected work both finished and in progress. After lunch they discussed the tasks ahead. They were apparently well satisfied: the local newspaper, the *Stratford Herald*, quotes Lord Chesham as saying, 'A wonderful job is being done by people who are doing it for the love of it.'

In his report to the March meeting of the Restoration Committee, David Hutchings noted that there were

Very small numbers of volunteers except for a large party arranged for the visit of Lord Chesham. Enthusiastic and able members of the Midlands Branch of the Inland Waterways Association have carried out a remarkable amount of work including the fitting of the lock gates. These few devoted people are undoubtedly the backbone of our volunteer force and without them little progress would have been made.

In a newspaper interview published in April he acknowledged help from other sources, notably the Boy Scouts Association, the Civic Trust, Toc H and other branches of the IWA: 'We regularly have parties from the Derby and Burton-on-Trent areas, from London, Cambridge, Reading, Bristol and even France, Italy and Germany—but very few from Warwickshire.'

Emscote, carrying 23 tons of ballast and drawing 3ft 7in (109cm) reached Lowsonford at the end of March 1962—at 9.55pm in a snowstorm—and *Cut and Trust* No 2, dated April 1962, was able to announce that the canal would be open for navigation to Lowsonford by Easter, although there was still some tidying up to do. In 36.6 per cent of the available time,

34.4 per cent of the work on lock gates had been done, together with 38.4 per cent of the dredging.

Incidentally, the print run of *Cut and Trust* was increased from 750 for the first issue to 1,000 for the second, which gives some idea of the number of donors receiving it—they having helped to find the £12,000 spent in the first year's work.

9
Year Two—To Wilmcote and Beyond

As a result of the work which was ahead of schedule beyond Lowsonford, both on locks and dredging, the *Cut and Trust* issue of April 1962 expressed the hope that the navigation might be open to Wootton Wawen by the early summer. This is a total distance of 6 miles (9.6km) and 18 locks from Lapworth and if it could be achieved, restoration would then be about four months ahead of schedule. The hope was based on the fact that by April new top gates had been fitted at Locks 32, 33 and 34 below Lowsonford and a further new top gate was in position at Lock 35 at Yarningale. Additionally, the hired Priestman Cub drag-line had progressed about a mile (1.6km) from its starting point at Lowsonford to just above Lock 35 at Yarningale. From there, it had about another ⅔ mile (1km) to go to Preston Bagot where it would reach the point at which the hired 10RB drag-line had started. In the meantime, the 10RB had completed about 1½ miles (2.4km) of dredging beyond Preston Bagot and had about another ½ mile (800m) to go to reach Wootton Wawen where yet another drag-line had started work. This was a large Smith 21 supplied and operated by the RAF Airfield Construction Training Unit based at the nearby village of Wellesbourne, which at that time was still an RAF base. It can be seen that activity was feverish.

One of the reasons why dredging was proceeding so well along these stretches was that in many places it had proved possible to negotiate for the spoil to be dumped on the adjacent fields. Even so, it was often necessary to erect mudboard walls in the fields to keep the mud within the agreed distance from the hedge. The RAF developed an improved technique for this purpose by first erecting an earth embankment in the field, using field soil dug from a trench along the edge of what was to be the dumping area, and then dumping between the hedge and that embankment. Also, there was a price to be paid for the facility of dumping in fields. The first farmer to agree to it settled for a compensation payment of £80 per mile (1.6km) but the committee minutes of April 1962 expressed concern that the amount asked was becoming successively larger with each farm that became involved. Mr Hutchings was asked to fix an upper limit of £200 per mile (1.6km) for any future offer, this to cover the farmer breaking up, spraying and reseeding the area.

One exception to the agreement of farmers to the dumping of spoil in the adjoining fields was a short length above Lock 34 at Yarningale Common where not only was the facility of dumping refused but all access across the fields, even on foot, was prohibited. This caused some trauma in the progress of the Priestman Cub on its way to Lock 35. Just above Lock 34 the canal and its towpath are carried over a stream in a short cast-iron aqueduct. Over this aqueduct, the water channel is in a trough about 9ft (2.7m) wide and the towpath is in another trough about 3ft (1m) wide by the side of the channel. The stream is some 15–20ft (4.5–6m) below and to either side of the stream is a steep embankment that could not be traversed by the drag-line in order to regain the towpath on the other side. The drag-line could not retreat along the towpath to reach the road access at Lowsonford where it had started because to do so it would have to cross the 150yd (137m) stretch of liquid mud which it had perforce dumped on the towpath. It could not be taken out across the adjoining field because of the refusal of access, so the only way was across the aqueduct. There was some doubt as to whether the aqueduct would stand the 8 ton load, and there was the difficulty that the whole aqueduct was not much wider than the machine and only offered two narrow strips of cast iron, at the top of the water trough, to support it. The aqueduct was completely emptied of water and the mud scraped out to lighten the load. A Bailey bridge with a timber deck was laid across the top of the aqueduct by the Territorial Army Royal Engineers, Harborne, and the drag-line inched across this platform. There must have been considerable relief when it safely reached the other side and one wonders how much its owners and insurers knew of its adventures.

By June 1962 the Secretary of the Local Restoration Committee, Michael Fox, was worried about a number of matters. First, although dredging was now going well, lock repairs were falling behind. In a letter to the chairman, he pointed out that of the total work to be done, dredging was 49 per cent completed but lock repairs only 41 per cent completed, although 44.4 per cent of the available time had elapsed. But more importantly, he felt that management problems were beginning to appear which resulted partly from the fact that not all of the members of the Restoration Committee had made themselves familiar with what was going on.

This has been a barrier to informed discussion and has prevented us taking any real control of events . . . on many occasions we seem to have degenerated into a rubber stamp. I believe that we have failed also in our responsibility to our Canal Manager who has not received the guidance that he is entitled to expect. If we rubber stamp his proposals without offering any constructive criticism we shall have only ourselves to blame if things don't work out. Of course, his [the Canal Manager's] approach to the committee has not been all that it should have been; his reports are a jumble and show hasty and inadequate preparation. Information requested has not always been produced and when we have specified a procedure for the presentation of accounts it has been adhered to once and then forgotten. But have we earned the respect that is apparently lacking? I doubt it and would not be surprised if David regards us as a body with a high nuisance value and largely unaware of the difficulties which he is facing and, in his own way, overcoming. The Trust may quite possibly be wondering whether they ought to appoint their own Local Management Committee but why should we not reorganise ourselves and find some new and more conscientious members? Is it not time that the volunteers were represented on the Management Committee?

But this was not to be because the National Trust would not agree to the addition of several persons who were eventually put forward.

The hopes of having the canal open to Wootton Wawen by the summer of 1962 were not, in the end, fulfilled. At the August meeting of the Restoration Committee, David Hutchings reported that although dredging was complete to well past Wootton and lock wall repairs had been completed up to and including Lock 38, the last before Wootton, new bottom gates were still awaited for Locks 35, 36, 37 and 38. In the end, the last of these locks was not completed until the middle of October.

Another event of the summer of 1962 was that the National Trust's Priestman Cub drag-line suffered mechanical failure and had to be left at Lock 31, where there was good road access, to await a major overhaul. This particular machine never worked on the canal again for it was discovered that the overhaul would keep it out of action for too long. Turriff's, who had obtained it for the restoration in the first place, took it back and generously allowed the full £750 which had originally been paid for it. With the assistance of Brian Knight, a newer Mark 5 Priestman Cub was located and bought in late summer for £1,425 at a Ministry of Agriculture and Fisheries sale. This was five years old and, according to the minutes, had done 5,000 hours of work in two years.

In spite of one dredger being out of action for some time, dredging was going so well that by October, when the locks to Wootton Wawen were ready, dredging had been completed to the Odd Lock, No 39, over a mile (1.6km) beyond Wootton. The 3-mile (4.8km) pound between Locks 38 and 39 was filled and *Emscote* proceeded to Wootton Wawen Basin where the fifty-second meeting of the Restoration Committee was held on her towards the end of October.

Then, still loaded with 23 tons of ballast, she proceeded to Lock 39 where she arrived on 31 October. By this time, £21,300 had been spent of the £42,000 estimated, rather more than half the total length had been dredged and half the locks restored.

Work on the second long pound from Lock 39 to the top of the Wilmcote Flight was well under way before the pound above was filled. A drag-line had started at the top of Wilmcote in August and by early November had dredged more than half the pound, working 'up' the canal, back towards Lock 39. By the end of November the pound was completed, using both a 10RB and a 19RB drag-line from the Western Command Plant Troop of the Royal Engineers, which was based locally at Long Marston, together with the hired Priestman Cub and the National Trust's Cub.

Meanwhile, repairs to Lock 39 had been finished and it was now possible to fill the second long pound between Locks 39 and 40, the latter at the top of the Wilmcote Flight. *Emscote* reached Featherbed Lane Bridge at Wilmcote on 16 December 1962, but was denied the privilege of being the first boat to reach the top of the Wilmcote Flight because she would not go through the bridge. The original plan of reaching the top of the flight by March 1963 would have been beaten by over three months, but for this obstacle.

It will be recalled that Featherbed Lane Bridge at Wilmcote was the one which had nearly caused the abandonment of the canal. By this time, it had been rebuilt by the County Council but it was known that the earth movements which cracked the old bridge had also squeezed in the bridge abutments, thus reducing the clearance on the channel through it. The narrowest point, which was in the southern approach to the bridge, had already been cut back and rebuilt because the clearance there had been reduced to 6ft 4½in (1.94m), which was obviously inadequate. It had been realised that width under the bridge itself was suspect, but there had been reluctance to demolish and rebuild the whole length of the towpath retaining wall if this could be avoided. *Emscote* showed that it could not be avoided—she stuck and had to be taken back to above Lock 39 (part of the way backwards until she could be turned), the pound had to be drained again and the whole of the towpath wall rebuilt through the bridge. Canada Bridge, a farm accommodation bridge between Featherbed Lane and Lock 40, also had to be widened for similar reasons, though two small cabin cruisers squeezed through it early in 1963 to become the first powered boats to reach the top of the Wilmcote Flight.

Work on the Wilmcote Flight, Locks 40–50 inclusive, was also ahead of schedule, having been started well before the end of 1962. This was just as well, for when the dense undergrowth covering them was cleared, they were discovered to be in even worse condition than had been thought. The eleven lock chambers on this 1 mile (1.6km) flight are deeper than all the others on the canal and this is possibly part of the reason why their walls had moved to such an extent. In several, it could actually be seen that the walls were bowed, with the chamber narrower in the middle than at the ends. In Lock 50, which was one of the worst, the clearance between the copings at the narrowest point was only 6ft 9in (2.05m). Both walls of Lock 50 had to be demolished from end to end, and in Locks 47, 48 and 49 the whole of one wall, that on the towpath side, had to be removed. Most of the others in the flight required removal of at least part of one wall to restore sufficient width. At Lock 49 an error of judgement was made in that the bulge in the wall was not cut away to a sufficient distance below water level: when the canal was reopened some of the deeper-draught boats became wedged on the ridge that was left, unless the pound below was kept artificially high by boards across the weir-crest. The demolitions revealed evidence that several had already been rebuilt in the past, presumably for a similar reason. As early as October 1962 work on Locks 40, 41 and 42 had progressed sufficiently for new top gates to be in position, but such was the amount of work required on this flight that it not only continued all winter but throughout most of 1963 as well.

The winter of 1962–3 was the worst on record for almost 100 years and has not been equalled since. Temperatures dropped to below freezing point just after Christmas 1962 and, instead of thawing after a few days as is usual, the cold weather persisted. The average maximum for the first twenty days of January was under 32.5°F (0.5°C) and the average minimum for the same period was 25°F (−4°C). There was about a foot (30cm) of snow in early January with severe drifting and because it was so cold this snow remained, further falls adding to it during the month. Then, at the end of January, temperatures dropped to −2°F (−19°C, or 34 degrees of frost). This prolonged cold had spectacular effects and caused many problems. The River Avon froze and people could walk on it; it was even said that a small car had been driven on to it. The ice on the canal was 18in (45cm) thick and even a 1 ton drag-line bucket dropped from a height of 40ft (12m) could not break it. It was necessary to keep an open channel on the canal aqueducts to prevent the cast-iron troughs from cracking, but this proved almost impossible: on one particular night the open water created by removing the ice with power-saws refroze to a depth of 8in (20cm). In early February, temperatures rose a little but at night were still around 25° to 20°F (−4° to −7°C), which would normally be thought quite cold but seemed warm by comparison. There was another spell of low temperatures and it was not until the end of Feburary that a proper thaw started. All the snow from January and February was still lying, leading to the possibility of flooding when it melted. Fortunately, the thaw was slow and, with precautions such as lowering the pounds as far as possible, no flooding materialised on the canal. However, the weather had a severe effect on the restoration. Not only was labour diverted to minimise damage, such as by keeping the aqueducts clear, but dredging was impeded, concrete would not pour and tools would not penetrate the ground.

8 David Hutchings (on right) working on Lock 54, Stratford, in heavy rain in late March 1963. The insubstantial working platform and its method of suspension can be seen

9 Dredging the Bancroft Basin, Stratford, October 1963

10 and 11 Before and after. The canal at the Lapworth end, just above Dick's Lane: (*above*) in 1960; (*below*) in 1964

10

Forward to Stratford

At this point in the narrative we have two rare and valuable documents: written reports to the Restoration Committee by the Canal Manager, David Hutchings. They are reproduced more or less verbatim with only a few slight alterations to make them more intelligible to those who do not know the canal as intimately as did the restoration manager and some of the committee.

Report by David Hutchings on Progress to Late March 1963
DREDGING. The canal has now been dredged once, twice, or three times [see later in chapter], except for the following sections. 1) Between Locks 42 and 50, a distance of about ½ mile [800m, most of the Wilmcote Flight]. 2) The northern end of Pound 50/51, a length of about 400yds [365m, Bishopton]. 3) A portion of Pound 51/52, a length of about 250yds [230m, outskirts of Stratford]. 4) Pound 52/53, a length of about 450yds [410m, Birmingham Road to Maidenhead Road, Stratford]. 5) Pound 55/56 [the approach to the Bancroft Basin].

A 19RB and occasionally a 10RB from the Royal Engineers at Long Marston are dredging down the Wilmcote Flight, the Royal Engineers from Southampton will deal with the portion of 50/51 next month and our Priestman Cub is finishing off Pound 51/52, although the winding hole immediately north of Lock 52 [Birmingham Road, Stratford] will be dealt with by a Smith 21 from the RAF at Wellesbourne. The delay in dredging Pound 52/53 is being caused entirely by the Ministry of Transport, who have not yet agreed to meet the cost under the terms of an agreement—the pound has been filled by road silt via a drain from the A34 Birmingham Road. The Town Clerk of Stratford and I have been in correspondence with the Ministry since last October [Stratford council being the road agent in this case]. Up to the time of writing neither I nor the Town Clerk have received a reply. The dredging of the northern end of Pound 55/56 will take place immediately heavy dumper trucks are available and I hope that these will be supplied by the United States Third Air Force with whom I am now in correspondence. The dredging of the basin will be postponed until the autumn.

Some difficulties have been encountered with the dumping and disposal of mud from the pounds inside Stratford but the situation is now satisfactory. [Much of it had to go on the towpath: for a long time after the reopening the towpath here was high above the water line, but most of it has now been cut down and levelled.] It is hoped that a second 19RB will be brought in from Western Command Plant Troop and this will be used to clear winding holes in the canal, deal again with already dredged sections where further dredging is necessary and eventually, with other drag-lines, to clear the basin in Stratford.

Much time and labour is still being used to clear trees and dense undergrowth from the Wilmcote Flight so that the drag-lines may move.

LOCKS. Apart from minor works such as painting, paddle gear adjustments, etc., all work has been completed to Lock 40. On the Wilmcote Flight, i.e. Locks 40 to 50, all the old lock gates, paddles and paddle starts have been removed, 8 new gates are in position and the demolishing and rebuilding of the walls of Lock 40 has begun. The new top gate of Lock 51 [Bishopton] has been installed, as have the paddle starts and paddles. The lock walls, overflow weir, etc. are now being demolished and rebuilt by prisoners from Winson Green Gaol in Birmingham. The condition of the walls of this lock is more serious than any we have yet encountered. It will be necessary to entirely demolish, for its full length and full height, the off-side wall together with the down-stream approach wall: large areas of the towing-path side wall and approach wall will also have to be demolished and rebuilt.

The top gate of Lock 52 has been installed and will be fitted shortly, the new paddle starts have been installed and the lock chamber dredged. The old bottom gate has been removed. The top gate of Lock 53 [Maidenhead Road, Stratford] has been installed together with new paddle starts, the old bottom gate removed and the lock chamber dredged. The new bottom gate will arrive next Thursday. The old gates of Lock 54 have been removed and both new gates installed, the top gate has been fitted together with new paddle starts and paddles. Work on the demolishing and rebuilding of the chamber walls is almost complete. Most of the mud and debris has been cleared from the lock chamber. More metal scrap—

including 18 bicycles—and other deposited rubbish has been found in this lock than in all the other locks combined. The overflow weir of this lock had, many years ago, been covered with corrugated iron and about four feet [1.2m] of dredgings dumped on top of that. This iron had rusted through and collapsed and therefore it has been necessary to completely dig out the spoil for the full length of the weir. New side walls are now being built.

The old gates of Lock 55 [Warwick Road] have been removed and new gates installed, the top gate has been fitted and work on the lock chamber above water level is now completed. Work on this lock cannot be finished until the level of water in Pound 55/56, which includes the Bancroft Basin, can be lowered.

The four gates of Locks 54 and 55 were measured, made, delivered and installed in ten days; a record for the project. Access to these two locks is particularly difficult and the bottom gates were the longest that have yet been made. It was necessary to use two cranes to install the bottom gate of Lock 55 and that of 54 was 'floated' in the canal and winched into position. 16ft [4.8m] stop planks, i.e. twice the normal length, have been made and are waiting to be installed at Lock 56, the barge lock from the basin to the river.

LABOUR. More volunteers are now arriving and the largest party this year, of about 9 persons, came last weekend from the Staffordshire and Worcestershire Canal Society. Six 'star' prisoners from Birmingham gaol have just started working on the canal [in early April] and it is planned that they shall work an 8-hour day for 6 days a week. We provide transport. [An old van had been bought for £169 for the purpose.] The Prison Commission hopes to extend this scheme after the initial problems have been overcome. The Port Handling Regiment from Marchwood, Southampton, is coming next month to deal with Lock 50 and the undredged section immediately below it. Arrangements are now being made to receive parties of volunteers throughout the summer, starting at Easter.

GENERAL. Apart from obstructions caused by ice in the recent cold weather, the canal has been navigable to Lock 40 since December 1962. It was intended that the canal should be navigable to this lock by the end of March 1963. The other work mentioned in this report is, in fact, in the third year's programme; i.e. March 63 to March 64.

The report mentions dredging taking place once, twice, or even three times, and this requires some explanation. When dredging first started in 1961 it was largely the dredger driver's decision as to what method he used since he already had drag-line experience (though not on canals) and no one else knew much about it. Most of this early work involved dumping spoil on the towpath behind mud-boards and when the driver had filled the available space he moved on. Although what appeared to be a reasonably deep channel was opened up down the centre of the canal by this means, quite a wide margin of untouched mud was often left to either side of this central channel. At the time, and judging by the amount of mud being piled on the towpath, it was thought that a sufficient quantity was being removed, but at a later stage it was realised that it had not been enough in some places. By 1963, dredging was being done routinely to a higher standard of width and depth of channel at the first pass, and second or even third runs became necessary to bring the earlier dredged sections up to the same standard.

Another factor which led to the need for redredging was the presence of water in the working area at the time of first dredging. Residual water was always present even after a pound had been drained for dredging, but if dredging could start from the bottom end of a pound and proceed 'upstream', most of this water could flow to and through the lock below, thus leaving the working area reasonably free of water. Unfortunately, it was not always possible to dredge in an upstream direction. If the mud had to be dumped on the towpath, then the dredger had to proceed away from the mud since it could not work upon or cross the recently dumped semi-liquid mud. Thus, if the only access to a particular pound was part-way along it, or worse still at the bottom end of it, then that part of the pound lying upstream of the access had to be dredged first, starting at the top and working back in a downstream direction towards the point where the machine could leave the towpath. Under these conditions the untouched mud further down the pound prevented the water from flowing away from the dredging site and the drag-line bucket was working in 2–3ft (61–91cm) of water. The operator could not see the depth, shape or boundaries of the channel being dug. Furthermore, an appreciable quantity of silt became stirred into the water and settled out again later in the area already dredged. Finally, the mud removed was of a much more fluid consistency and so more difficult to pile up when dumped. These limitations had to be accepted and such areas redredged later.

Of all the problems associated with dredging, disposal of the mud was the most difficult. The technique of dumping on the towpath behind mud-boards, as already described, was not very satisfactory. Apart from the considerable labour requirement for installing and recovering the boards, there was a severe limitation on the amount of mud that could be contained. By 1963 a method had been devised for dumping on reasonably wide parts of the towpath without the use of mud-boards. First, the drag-line was used to remove the top layer of the towpath to form a wide trench, the soil from this being placed in a steep bank at the edge of the channel. On a second pass the trench thus formed was filled with the dredged mud. However, this method was not thought advisable for use on embankments in case disturbance of the towpath subsoil increased the risk of bank leakage.

Experience showed that it was feasible to overfill the towpath trench, relying on shrinkage of the mud to reduce its volume. In time, it dried and consolidated to about half its original bulk and when this had happened redredging became possible. For ease of walking, it was desirable to level out the dredged material soon after it dried as otherwise even the minor heaps tended to become permanent. To reduce this problem it was important to move the drag-line frequently, even as often as yard by yard. Although the machine could dredge quite considerable lengths from one station, the result of doing so was to produce great mounds of spoil at certain points along the towpath with valleys between the mounds.

Difficulties of access were also mentioned in the report.

The canal authority (in this case the National Trust) was and is empowered by the act of parliament under which the canal was constructed, to use land adjacent to the canal for the purpose of access for maintenance. This right was never enforced by the National Trust, except in the case of the Bancroft Basin, preference being given to negotiation. Particular difficulty over access was experienced between Maidenhead Road Lock (No 53) and Warwick Road Lock (No 55) in Stratford. Because of these two road bridges which cross both the canal and its towpath by confining them to what is, in effect, a short tunnel it was not possible for a drag-line to reach this stretch via the towpath. Also, there is no other access which is both possible for a large and heavy drag-line and which lies solely over canal land. Ironically, there is a considerable area of land on the towpath side by Lock 54 which belongs to the canal, but there is no right of access to it from a road. The easiest access would have been across the derelict site of some demolished cottages alongside Maidenhead Road but this site belonged to the Borough Council, who were still against the restoration and refused permission. Access was eventually gained across a private garden with the owner's permission, but he stipulated a maximum period of two weeks so that the hedge and garden shrubs which had to be moved could be replanted quickly, before the spring. The dredging was done and four lock gates replaced within the time specified, thus creating the record noted by Mr Hutchings in his report.

Report by David Hutchings on Progress to mid-June 1963

All of the present work on the canal, except for essential maintenance or improvements, is concentrated on the Wilmcote Flight and Lock 51 directly below it.

The work of the third and final year comprises the opening of the section between Lock 40 at the top of the Wilmcote Flight and the River Avon in Stratford. The third year period began on April 1st. This work involves the restoration of 17 locks and the dredging of about $1\frac{1}{2}$ miles [2.4km] of canal.

LOCKS. Of the 17 locks, at least 8 have to be very extensively repaired and in some cases virtually rebuilt. One or both of the lock walls and the approach walls have to be completely demolished and new walls built. This very serious set-back was not suspected until precise dimensions were taken, when it was found that walls had been pushed or had fallen inwards and thus the lock chambers had been narrowed to a degree which is unacceptable. The causes of the distortion probably include:

1 Side-ground pressures against walls which have for many years been unsupported by water, i.e. the ground pressures have not been countered by the water pressure which exists in a full lock.
2 The almost complete lack of ties between the facing work and the main wall structure (where elm ties did exist they have almost invariably failed).
3 Frost action during many winters and particularly last winter.
4 Possible settlement of the foundations which are based on the clay of the Wilmcote area. This settlement may be due to the fact that some of the pounds have been dry for many years.

The following method of wall construction is being used. The faulty wall is being demolished for virtually its full height and to a depth into the wall sufficient to reveal sound work: this is up to 4ft [1.2m] in some cases. Pneumatic hammers and, where necessary, explosives are being used to remove the faulty masonry. The face of the sound work is cleaned with hoses, airlines and wire brushes, the top and bottom quoins are reset and shuttering is then erected on the new line of the wall. Heavy mesh reinforcement is erected for the full length and height of the wall and concrete is poured. About 4ft [1.2m] below coping level a 'continuous' steel bar is laid horizontally and fastened to the mesh reinforcement, heavy steel anchorbars are hooked around the horizontal tie and the other ends of the anchor bars are then encased in 4ft [1.2m] cubes of concrete which are set as far back from the lock wall as is possible.

These methods have been discussed with British Waterways Board Engineers[1] who came to inspect the work a few days ago, with Mr Thomas of the Ministry of Transport and with Dr Boucher, a highly qualified and experienced civil engineer. All these gentlemen have expressed themselves satisfied with the methods being

---

[1] The national canal system was by now controlled by the British Waterways Board (see Chapter 15).

adopted and with the quality of the work, except Mr Thomas who has not yet replied to my letters.

The situation so far as locks are concerned is that: Locks 50 and 54 are completed except for very minor items, e.g. the fitting of bumping plates to the gates. Lock 55 is about 60 per cent completed. Lock 51, which is a particularly difficult case, is about 60 per cent completed, as is Lock 49. Lock 48 is about 20 per cent completed and Lock 40 is about 40 per cent completed. Work has begun on all the other locks in the year's programme, although in some cases this only comprises the removal of the lock gates and paddle starts and installation of new ones: – except for Lock 56, the barge lock into the river. The quoins of the rebuilt locks are being reset to 7ft 6in [2.28m] across the top for the top gate and 7ft 9in [2.36m] across the top for the bottom gate; and 7ft 3 or 4in [2.20–2.23m] across the bottom, for both gates.

DREDGING. Of the 1½ mile [2.4km] section concerned, the following work remains to be done: – The dredging of Pound 52/53 which has been delayed by the necessity to negotiate with the Ministry of Transport, who have now agreed to contribute £120 to the cost. Also to be done, about half of Pound 50/51, which includes the basin; and various short stretches of the Wilmcote Flight. At present no drag-lines are working on this section. Our own Priestman Cub is engaged on improving Pound 38/39, where a number of minor scours are being removed to facilitate the operation of the passenger-carrying narrow boat *Linda* which is now based at Wootton Wawen. This work will be completed by the end of the current week and the drag-line will then be brought onto the Wilmcote Flight. The Royal Engineers' 10RB is in constant use as a crane and is proving particularly valuable for the removal of masonry and mud from the lock chambers, coping stones from the tops of the walls and for the installation of new lock gates.

LABOUR. We are very fortunate indeed to have been able to obtain labour from the Prison Commissioners. Without this help, which at present comprises an average of a dozen prisoners a day, there would be little hope of completing the programme on time. Even so, it must be clearly understood that there is still a very definite danger that work will take longer than originally expected, although no effort will be spared to ensure that the canal is navigable by the original agreed opening date. It is hoped that the size of parties from Winson Green Gaol will be increased and a single-deck ex-London Transport omnibus has now been bought to transport extra prisoners between the prison and the canal.

FINANCE. We have spent about £36,000 and there is £5,000 of the originally estimated sum still available, together with a supplementary £7,000. Whether this will be sufficient depends very much on the cost of work on the basin. The locks more or less completed so far have cost an average of £550 each, of which more than £400 is for the new gates and paddle starts. Those on the Wilmcote Flight may each cost 40 per cent more than this average.

David Hutchings' financial report requires some amplification. The total sum needed had originally been estimated at £42,000; £22,000 to come from public subscription and £20,000 as a grant from the Ministry of Transport. The £36,000 spent comprised about £19,000 from the subscription source plus about £17,000 from the grant, paid on a pro rata basis in the proportion of the totals. This left something over £5,000 available out of the originally estimated amount, from the two sources combined. However, the public appeal had been oversubscribed and stood nominally at £29,000 rather than at £22,000, thus forming the 'supplementary £7,000' referred to.

The report also mentions that an increasing number of prisoners from Winson Green Gaol in Birmingham were now working on the canal. A tale told to the author, concerning a conversation that took place at the time with one of the warders who accompanied the prisoners, suggests that at the outset only a few prisoners showed any interest in volunteering for such work parties and then only on the basis that it might provide a soft option. The initial reaction of the majority was apparently unprintable. By the time prison work parties had been operating regularly for some time, most of them were not only working quite hard, provided that they were supervised, but also taking some pride in the work—so much so that the original volunteers were said to be 'vetting' the now long waiting list of applicants and recommended to the warders those that they thought likely to measure up to the standards.

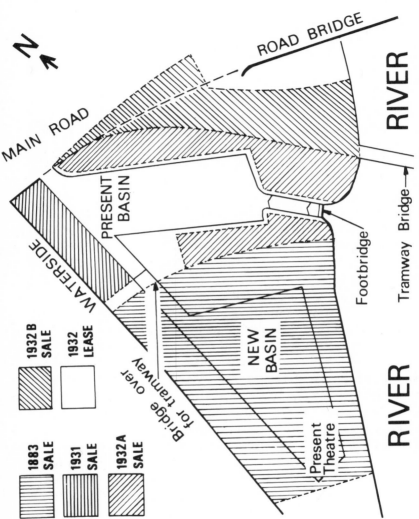

Fig 2   The Bancroft Basin and Gardens, Stratford-upon-Avon

11

Battles of the Bancroft Basin

Before moving on to the restoration of the basin in the Bancroft Gardens in Stratford, it is worth taking a look at the previous history of that area, partly for its own interest but particularly because it helps in the understanding of the battle which developed.

Immediately prior to 1883, the Great Western Railway owned the whole of the Bancroft area as covered by Fig 2, having taken over the West Midland Railway Company, into which had been amalgamated the Oxford Worcester & Wolverhampton Railway (the 'Old Worse & Worse') which itself had bought the canal and its associated land in the Bancroft area from the Company of Proprietors of the Stratford-upon-Avon Canal Navigation in 1857. There were still two basins in 1883, surrounded by an ugly and squalid collection of premises which included ten coal wharves, a lead and glass wharf, a cider press, a cooperage, a skin yard and a timber yard. The whole area was served by a network of tramway lines. The original theatre, still standing at that time, was further down the bank of the River Avon than is the present one and thus beyond the above site.

In 1883, the 'Mayor Aldermen and Burgesses of the Borough of Stratford-upon-Avon' (known as 'the Corporation') purchased from the GWR the southern part of the site, being the triangular 'New Basin', as it was known, and its surrounds (marked with vertical hatching in Fig 2). The purchase was freehold but subject to a covenant that the area was to be used only as public walks and pleasure grounds. The coal wharves and other premises along the town side (Waterside) edge of the New Basin were demolished, the basin filled in, trees planted and the area landscaped as gardens. The present basin remained, together with its associated wharves, premises and tramways, although in 1894 the GWR agreed with the Corporation that part of the tramway system could be used as public walks connecting the Tramway Bridge over the Avon with the 1883 'gardens' purchase.

In 1931, the area between the present basin and Waterside, marked by horizontal hatching in Fig 2, was bought by the Corporation from the GWR for £2,543. Under covenants, a narrow strip was to be incorporated into the public highway (Waterside) and the remainder used for public pleasure gardens only. The premises on this area were also demolished and the land tidied up. It should be noted that this sale did not include a narrow strip between the 1883 and 1931 purchases, which gave access to the basin and its surrounding land from Waterside, at the point where the tramway system crossed the now partly filled-in cut originally connecting the two basins (the 'lily arm', as it is sometimes called locally).

The original theatre had burnt down in 1926 and by now work had started on the new one, largely sited on the southern end of the New Basin area involved in the 1883 sale, which was still under the 'public walks and pleasure grounds only' covenant. By this time, the canal and the remaining basin had largely fallen into disuse and in 1932 the latter became the subject of several transactions. These resulted from a complex set of agreements made in 1929 between the GWR, the Shakespeare Memorial Theatre (as it then was) and the Corporation. The GWR agreed to sell to the theatre the two areas surrounding the present basin (marked by diagonal hatching in Fig 2—1932A and 1932B), and to lease to the theatre the basin itself and some land immediately bordering it (left clear in Fig 2). The whole of this deal was for a payment of £2,500. Simultaneously, the theatre agreed to transfer to the Corporation the 1932A area around the basin, together with the lease of the basin area, in exchange for the site on which the present-day theatre stands. The theatre also agreed to sell to the Corporation the 1932B area for £2,500—the same amount that they had paid to the GWR for the whole deal. The rather strange curving boundaries of these various pieces of land result from delineation of the boundaries by the routes followed by the tramways.

It is no longer obvious why the deal was done in this complicated manner, but it was probably connected with the fact that 'the Theatre' and 'the Corporation' largely comprised the same individuals wearing different hats. The overall result was that the Corporation paid £2,500 and became the owners of all the land surrounding the basin and lessees of the basin and its immediate perimeter, while the theatre became the owner of its present site, apparently at no cost. In the same transactions, the GWR released the theatre site (but that alone) from the covenant concerning use as public pleasure gardens only. Since this release was dated February 1932 and the theatre was opened in April of that year, the new theatre must have been built before its building became legally permissible.

All of the additional land taken into ownership by the Corporation in 1932 was freehold. The 1932B part was to be used partly to widen the main road at Bridgefoot, partly as public walks (tramway) and the rest 'as required by the Corporation', provided that its use was not prejudicial to the interests of the GWR in the use of the basin. The 1932A part was to be used only as public pleasure gardens. (There was also a tiny isolated piece of the gap between the 1883 and 1931 purchases, but not marked on the plan, which was to be incorporated into the road called Waterside).

The area leased to the Corporation (and now vested in the Stratford-on-Avon District Council) is '1 acre, 1 rood, 30 perches and one-quarter perch or thereabouts'. It comprises firstly the basin itself, the lock and the remains of the canal arm that had led to the other basin. It also includes a narrow strip of land on both sides of the lock and along all but the Waterside edge of the basin (approximately the paths now alongside the basin); a roughly diamond-shaped area by the arm which was designated as a wharf; and access to all of this from Waterside through the gap between the 1883 and 1931 purchases. The lease is for 1,000 years from 25 December 1931, at an annual rent of 10s (50p).

The lease is subject to a number of conditions, the most important (from the canal point of view) being as follows:

1   The Corporation was, at its own expense and to the approval of the GWR engineer (a) to construct such works as it might require in order to use part as ornamental gardens; (b) to maintain the wharf and the access thereto; (c) to maintain the basin as ornamental water.

2   The GWR and any others with legitimate claims had the right of access to the leased area to work and maintain the lock and pass vessels through it; and to load and unload vessels and pass them through the basin. In other words, the right to continue use of the basin, wharf and lock as part of the canal.

3   The lock and its paddles were to be maintained by the GWR.

4   The Corporation was not to (a) impede traffic on the canal or damage the walls of the basin; (b) place any advertisement or placard other than byelaws on any part of the land or premises; (c) assign the lease without the agreement of the GWR.

Yet another series of agreements dealt with the bridge by the lock. This was originally a tramway swing bridge over the tail of the lock which, by 1904, had fallen into disrepair. In that year the Corporation was allowed to construct, own and maintain a replacement footbridge, provided that it had sufficient headroom for the passage of boats. In 1934 the Corporation was allowed to replace the 1904 bridge by a lower one over the lock itself (without headroom for boats) 'for greater convenience of access to the gardens'.

Since 1932, only nominal changes have occurred in the

ownership of the Bancroft area. When the railways were nationalised in 1948, the canal passed to the British Transport Commission. At the beginning of restoration in 1960 the National Trust took over the canal from the BTC, first on a temporary basis and later permanently, thus becoming the 'canal authority' and inheriting the covenants and lessor's rights originally set up by the GWR. At the time of restoration, the Stratford-upon-Avon Borough Corporation was still the owner and lessee of the various parts of the Bancroft area, but on the 1974 reorganisation of local government the area passed to the Stratford-on-Avon District Council who, of course, also inherited all the conditions and obligations as well. The only other point of note is that at some time prior to the start of restoration the Corporation attempted to buy the basin instead of leasing it, so that it could close the canal, but the BTC would not agree.

Situated as it is, in the middle of the riverside gardens by the theatre in the heart of tourist Stratford, the Bancroft Basin had been a bone of contention ever since the beginning of the restoration campaign. As early as June 1959, just after the failure of the County Council's application for a warrant to abandon the canal, the *Stratford Herald* carried an article headed 'Objection to mooring in the Bancroft Canal Basin'. Stratford council had received a letter from the Inland Waterways Redevelopment Board which stated:

The committee fully appreciate your council's natural desire that the basin in the Bancroft Gardens should be preserved as a very special amenity . . . but . . . they feel that if the canal were redeveloped for pleasure craft it would be difficult and undesirable wholly to prevent the use of the basin.

The River and Recreation Grounds Committee of the council

. . . objected strongly to any proposal whereby the basin might become a mooring base and the Planning Committee agreed to write to the Inland Waterwasy Redevelopment Committee strongly opposing any such scheme.

Objection to the potential presence of boats in the basin was not the only problem. A new road bridge over the River Avon at Stratford had been under discussion since 1862 and although it has still not materialised at the time of writing, its construction was supposedly imminent when restoration of the Bancroft Basin was about to start. The official proposal from the road planners included a completely new canal pound, to be cut from the tail of Lock 55 (Warwick Road) to the Avon, coming out somewhere around the present site of the Hilton Hotel. This 'New Cut', as it became known, was to enable the access roads to the new bridge to cross the old line of the canal at low level between Lock 55 and the basin, the new bridge itself lying by the side of the old. For Stratford council, this proposal had the additional appeal that it would once and for all prevent boats from appearing in the Bancroft Basin. From the start of negotiations both the Local Restoration Committee and the National Trust agreed to accept the alternative New Cut, provided that it had the same facilities as the original route—that is, fully reinforced banks, a basin and a 14ft wide (4.2m) lock into the Avon—and provided that it was finished by 1 March 1964 on which date the canal was due to reopen.

On 20 July 1962 a meeting on the subject was held in Stratford Town Hall between representatives of the Ministry of Transport, the County Council, British Transport Waterways, the National Trust, the Local Restoration Committee and the Stratford Urban District Council. A ministry representative was the main speaker and it emerged that while the ministry was prepared to build a new cut and lock, neither it nor anyone else wanted to pay for a new basin. The minutes of the subsequent meeting of the Restoration Committee record that 'The ministry had not realised there would be all these difficulties.' In October 1962 the Restoration Committee's Acting Chairman, Mr King, wrote to the Ministry of Transport requesting that a definite date be stated for the construction of the New Cut: it was not forthcoming.

12 Brian Knight fitting the new top gates of the barge lock from the Bancroft Basin into the river, November 1963. Stop planks are in position both above and below the lock and two pumps are keeping down the level of the water seeping into the lock

13 Test cruise by *Emscote*: in the pound below Lock 50 at the bottom of the Wilmcote flight. 31 May 1964 — only six weeks before the reopening ceremony

14 Her Majesty Queen Elizabeth the Queen Mother arriving at the barge lock in the Bancroft Basin, Stratford, for the reopening ceremony, 11 July 1964

In January 1963 David Hutchings and J. F. W. Rathbone, Secretary of the National Trust, met again with Stratford Borough Council who formally requested that the Bancroft Basin and its lock be excluded from the reopening of the canal. They asked that the Trust should instead rely on the provision of a new cut. Following this meeting, Mr Hutchings received instructions from the Trust's Head Office that he was not to begin any work in the Bancroft Gardens until agreement had been reached between the Trust and the Council—despite the fact that such work had originally been scheduled for the early part of 1963. This was a major concession to the council since, under the terms of the lease, the canal authority (now the Trust) was entitled to access for work. The sensitivity of the council on the whole subject is illustrated by a letter sent about that time by the town clerk to Mr Hutchings.

It has been brought to my notice that this morning a Land-Rover was driven along the tramway footpath and over the canal foot-bridge into the Bancroft Gardens, leaving by Waterside. A member of the Parks Department ascertained from the driver of the vehicle that this incident was a preliminary inspection prior to cranes soon being brought up to remove the existing lock gates. It would appear that this matter has some connection with the Canal Committee's activities. If so, I feel that I should bring to your attention the fact that there is no right to make a vehicular approach to this lock over Corporation land without the express consent of the Corporation.

By this time, it was obvious that the New Cut could not be constructed in time for the reopening of the canal in the early summer of 1964. The New Cut was still only a proposal; it had not yet received the parliamentary sanction which would be needed and it could not do so until the plans for the new bridge were themselves finalised. Clearly, the New Cut would not be ready for several years, at best. The main point to be considered in relation to this was that the National Trust had taken the canal for a trial period of five years, which ended on 28 September 1965, and by then it had to decide whether to retain the canal indefinitely or return it to the British Waterways Board (as it had now become). The decision would have to be based on operating experience in 1964 because notice of intention was required by March 1965 and this experience would only be meaningful if maximum utilisation, and thus maximum revenue, was obtained. Maximum utilisation could only occur if access to and from the river was available. It was also considered that much of the national impact of the reopening would be lost if 'the VIP concerned' (the identity was secret at that stage) could not voyage out on to the river to join up with the Shakespeare quatercentenary celebrations. Finally, Stratford was the proposed venue for the 1964 National Boat Rally of the Inland Waterways Association, to celebrate the restoration, and if the basin and lock to the river were not open there would be no suitable site.

The Restoration Committee unanimously recommended that 'The opening of the canal to the River Avon should not be postponed beyond the original date of March 1964' and in February 1963 the Executive Committee of the National Trust formally agreed. This meant, of course, that restoration of the original Bancroft Basin and its lock must go ahead. What a wise decision that was: we would still be waiting for the New Cut today. A letter sent by the National Trust to the town clerk of Stratford to inform him of the decision, added the following:

Any damage for which we [the NT] are liable will of course be put right by us. Furthermore, with voluntary labour which we may have available it may be possible to help you with repairs to the basin walls, for which of course we are not legally liable.

A press statement was also issued, explaining the reasons for the decision and the efforts being made by the Trust to co-operate with Stratford Borough Council.

Some of the members of the Local Restoration Committee felt that the National Trust was being far too co-operative with the council. They argued that since, under the terms of the lease, the council was responsible for maintenance of the basin and since the basin had not been properly maintained, the Trust was entitled to do whatever was necessary and charge the cost to the council. The chairman wrote to the Trust asking for clarification of policy and suggesting that the Restoration Committee should itself negotiate directly with the council.

However, it was apparently thought best to keep the by now somewhat militant Local Restoration Committee out of the negotiations with the council, since they heard nothing further from the Trust on this matter. On 14 June the *Stratford Herald* reported that an agreement had been reached between representatives of the National Trust and the Borough Council at a meeting which had taken place in London on 29 May. At this meeting it was again stated that Stratford council did not want the Bancroft Basin used by boats, for two reasons: first, the possible loss of amenity values to the Memorial Theatre Gardens; second, it was not fair to the ratepayers to charge them between £10,000 and £15,000 for reopening the basin. The Trust restated its intention of opening the canal to the Avon by the spring of 1964 and offered compromises, which were confirmed two days later in a letter from the secretary of the Trust to the town clerk of Stratford council.

We agreed that it would be unreasonable to expect your council to bear the full cost of repairing the basin's walls if the Bancroft Basin is only to be used for navigation on a temporary basis. The Trust is accordingly prepared to meet the cost of any repairs to the basin's walls which it considers are necessary for temporary navigation on the understanding that this will be repaid to the Trust by the council if a new cut and basin acceptable to the Trust are not provided within, say, three years and the present basin remains in navigational use. The Trust is further prepared to demolish the existing footbridge over Lock 56 and to provide a new bridge of a type and design and on a site satisfactory to both of us. Lock 56 will be rebuilt and equipped by the Trust with four new gates and new paddles. This also will be paid for by the Trust, although again on the same understanding.

A thorough inspection was first needed, which would mean draining the basin. It was suggested that a council representative should accompany Mr Hutchings during this inspection, but it was stated that the final decision on how repair work should be carried out rested with the Trust.

A press release summarising the above was also issued by the Trust and it was on this that the press report of 14 June was based. That report also stated that the Highways and Sewerage Committee, who were responsible for the basin, would recommend the council to approve the proposals on condition that the council was not liable for the cost of the lock. This proviso was presumably because, under the terms of the lease, the lock was the only thing for which the council was *not* responsible. The chairman and vice-chairman of the Highways and Sewerage Committee were named as the representatives for the inspection.

The Restoration Committee had no prior knowledge that any discussions were taking place, much less that an agreement had been reached, but by coincidence a committee meeting had been fixed for the very day on which the agreement was reported in the press. At that meeting Mr Hutchings gave details of the discussions, at which he had been present, and stated that the newspaper report differed in some respects from his own understanding of the agreement. It was minuted that 'As no member of the committee had received a report from the National Trust, it was not possible to resolve this difference'. It was also minuted that 'several members expressed dissatisfaction with the lack of consultation with the committee'. They firmly believed that, as they had been appointed as the Trust's Local Management

Committee, they had the right to be both heard and kept informed.

As well as this concern over the principles involved, members of the Local Management Committee were also at variance with the terms of the agreement itself. Mr Hutchings wrote to the National Trust saying that he was not at all happy with it, particularly because the Trust had relieved the council of all its responsibilities and had shouldered them itself. Mr Fox wrote to express concern as to where the extra money for the work on the basin was to be found. He suggested that, on the basis of the figures supplied to the committee by Mr Hutchings, the canal work itself, without the basin would swallow £49,600 expenditure from a fund which stood at a maximum of £49,000, even taking into account the oversubscription.

The incident revealed that several members of the Restoration Committee were becoming disillusioned about the whole relationship between it and the National Trust. The chairman wrote to Mr Rathbone as follows:

At our last committee meeting we learned—and then only from newspaper reports—of the Trust's meeting with the Town Council. I believe that at our meeting the morale of the committee was at its lowest, because it seemed to be the general opinion that our meetings were a waste of time in that all the members received was a progress report from the canal manager, over whom there is no control, either financial or otherwise, and that the committee is ignored in all matters of any importance.

The minutes which recorded the various expressions of dissatisfaction were also automatically circulated to the two representatives of the Trust who were co-opted members of the Canal Society Committee but who had not been present at that particular meeting. At the next meeting, in September, the Trust was represented by both Mr Rathbone and Mr Burr, and the former explained the Trust's decision. Hindsight suggests that the Trust was probably right. Stratford council was in such an intransigent mood about the basin that it would probably have been necessary to resort to litigation to make it discharge its responsibilities under the lease. This would have taken far too long and would have further soured relations with the council.

The meeting decided that an estimate for a replacement footbridge should be obtained; that after inspection a decision should be made on the minimum work necessary to make the basin temporarily navigable for three years; and that complete records be kept of cost so that it could be reclaimed from the council as agreed, if the basin was still in use after three years. It is, of course, still in use to this day but no record has come to light to indicate that the Trust has ever received, or even asked for, reimbursement from the council. In this context it is interesting to note that in 1977, after the Bancroft Basin and Gardens had been transferred to the Stratford-on-Avon District Council following the reorganisation of local government, the District Council dredged the basin at its own expense, thereby tacitly accepting responsibility.

In pursuance of the National Trust's policy of co-operation with Stratford Borough Council, no work on the Bancroft Basin was started until the autumn of 1963, after the main tourist season had ended. On 16 September it was drained for inspection and the lock gates were removed and taken, as patterns for the new ones, to Messrs Wyckham Blackwell.

The draining revealed an unexpected feature in the presence of underwater remains of the old towpath under the Banbury Road Bridge where the canal enters the basin. These remains were not removed during the restoration and survive to this day as an underwater hazard to deeper-draught boats, particularly when the basin is low. They provide a slightly malicious diversion for the knowing boater moored in the basin, watching successive boats whose steerers have failed to read their canal guide going aground under the bridge. One day, perhaps, the remains could be used as the foundation for a restored towpath under the bridge so that visitors could follow the canal by walking up the towpath out of the basin (something which is not at present possible).

Prisoners from Birmingham and Maidstone gaols and volunteers began work on the basin and its lock on 14 October 1963. The dredging was done by a 19RB and two 10RB drag-lines from the Royal Engineers' Western Command Plant Troop, Long Marston, together with the Trust's Priestman Cub. An estimated 10,000 tons of mud was removed, loaded into seven tipper lorries loaned, gratis, by Messrs John Laing and driven by prisoners, and carted away to be spread as 'top cover' on the council's rubbish dump by the side of the river upstream of the town (more or less the site of the present swimming pool). To protect the surface of the Bancroft Gardens, the whole operation was carried out on 'roads' made from 1,000 railway sleepers laid around the basin and across the grass of the gardens. The council remained unco-operative and attempted to prevent access of plant to the basin even though the terms of its lease specifically allowed it. Although it was, at the time, importing soil to form a top-seal on its rubbish tip, initially it would not allow dredgings from the basin to be taken there for the same purpose. The story is widely held that it did not maintain this proviso after threats to dump all the dredgings in a mound in the disused and navigationally unwanted arm of the basin, right in the middle of the gardens.

Dredging of the basin proved particularly difficult because it is so wide that the drag-line buckets could not be swung to the centre and because it could not be drained completely. The fall of the lock into the river is small and when the river is at its normal level, as determined by the weir downstream by the church, the water level of the river is above the bottom level of the basin. Since it was not possible initially to lower the river level by opening the sluices, the deeper part of the dredging in the basin had to be done with the drag-line buckets working under water, thus preventing the operators from seeing what they were doing. To reach the ridge of mud in the middle a floating pontoon was built by the Western Command Plant Troop and one of their dredgers was operated from it.

Extensive repairs were needed on the walls of the basin and it was also necessary to build a new weir from the basin into the river. The original overflow weir for this pound had been at the far end of the second basin, filled in many years earlier. Since then, surplus water had flowed over the top of the gates of Lock 56, the barge lock into the river. This kept the water level in the basin about 9in (23cm) above the correct navigation level and left too little headroom for boats under the low bridge beneath the Banbury Road, between Lock 55 and the basin. The new weir, built alongside the lock and totally enclosed for safety, lowered the water to the correct level giving sufficient, though still restricted, headroom under the bridge. Unfortunately, the lowering of the water level had an unforeseen effect: it put an end to the model-boating which had previously been a popular feature of the basin because it was now difficult to reach down to the water from the basin walls.

In order to work on the lower part of the lock itself it was essential, as with all the others, to have it free of water. It was intended to achieve this by fitting stop-planks at the tail of the lock, between it and the river, and pumping the water out. However, it proved impossible to obtain a sufficiently good seal between the stop-planks and the bottom, and even frogmen were unable to remove the underwater debris causing the trouble. Water continued to seep back into the lock as fast as it was pumped out, although the pumps were removing some 100,000gal (450 decalitres) an hour. Permission had therefore to be obtained from the Severn River Authority (as it then was) to open the sluices at the weir at Lucy's Mill, further down the river. This was done on Saturday 8 November and by Sunday morning the river level was low enough to allow work to proceed. About 6ft (1.8m) of mud was removed from the bottom of the lock and the new bottom gates fitted; the sluices were closed early on Monday morning and by 10am that day the river was full again.

The new bottom gates were originally fitted with cranked beams to clear the new footbridge that was to be erected over the tail of the lock. However, these proved unsatisfactory in use because they gave insufficient leverage on the heavy gates and, shortly after the reopening of the canal, they were replaced by a mechanical gate-opening system operated by a windlass. Mechanical problems resulting from wear eventually forced the replacement of this system, and the gates now have cranked metal extensions.

By the end of November the dredging was finished, including the pound from Lock 55 into the basin; repair of the basin walls was almost complete and all four lock gates were in position, though the top ones still had to be fitted. Heavy rain during the work had partially nullified the protection to the ground afforded by the laying of railway sleepers and parts of the lawns had become a quagmire. A considerable amount of returfing was needed and even this was paid for out of canal restoration funds, although it had originally been understood that the council would meet the cost.

A design for the replacement footbridge had already been agreed between the National Trust and the council and this was constructed at Wormwood Scrubs Prison at a cost of £500. It was delivered on 29 December 1963 on a lorry freely loaned by Messrs John Laing, placed in position by a crane from the Royal Engineers' depot at Long Marston and installed, over the tail of the lock, by prisoners from Winson Green Gaol. The timber decking was put on this new bridge in February 1964 and the old concrete bridge, which spanned the lock chamber, was then removed.

The *Stratford Herald* of 29 November 1963 carried a full-page article about the basin and summarised the whole affair. It first quoted its own report of 1 March of that year to the effect that 'Every available means will be employed by

Stratford Town Council to induce the National Trust to desist from its repeated aim of providing canal access to the River Avon by March next year.' It then continued: 'So far the operations have provided an unfailing source of entertainment for Stratfordians and visitors alike. The work will soon be finished and as yet the dreaded spoilation of the gardens has not taken place.' On the other hand, at a Town Council meeting in mid-December, Alderman Mrs Waldron expressed her view that 'The abomination of desolation' of the Bancroft Basin was now being cleared up and she 'fervently hoped it would soon be back in order'. Reactions obviously varied, but the battles of the Bancroft were over. One suspects, however, that the war has continued to this day in the bitterness of some of the defeated parties.

12

The Final Push

While the controversy raged over the Bancroft Basin, other work continued, as the following reports reveal.

Report by David Hutchings on Progress to September 1963
GENERAL. It was discovered that 10, not 8 as previously thought, of the remaining 17 locks required extensive rebuilding, that is, 10 of the 12 locks which virtually constitute the Wilmcote Flight. [Lock 51 at Bishopton is presumably included here.] The time available for dealing with each lock was three weeks and as it had previously taken six weeks to reinstate locks which were in a far better state of repair it was obvious that extraordinary methods would have to be taken if the restoration programme were to be completed on time. Apart from the volume and the intricacy of the work, problems included difficult access, particularly during wet weather—and this summer has been wet—via which to cart away debris often amounting to over 200 tons per lock and to bring in materials for the new walls.

The situation has been saved almost entirely by the presence of prison labour from Winson Green Gaol as response to the many appeals for volunteers has been disappointing. Far fewer have arrived than in any of the previous years and although these, as usual, were normally members of the I.W.A., the response even from that association has been quite inadequate.

Work was started on Lock 40 [Wilmcote top] last winter but little could be done because of the weather. The main effort began at Lock 51 [Bishopton] at the beginning of April and has since progressed up the flight. Recently a party of Royal Engineers and Royal Pioneers from the Engineering Supply Depot at Long Marston began work at Lock 40 and will restore this lock and Lock 41, thus meeting the main working parties now moving on to Lock 42. Methods suitable for entirely unskilled and inexperienced labour have had to be evolved and speed has been a vital factor. As in previous years, work has continued 7 days a week and has never ceased even during the heaviest rain.

The situation now is as follows:

LOCKS. The following have been entirely reconstructed and new gates and paddles have been installed, and in some cases fitted: Nos 51, 50, 49, 48, 47, 46, 45, 44, 43, 40. In every case weirs have had to be rebuilt and every paddle start and paddle has been removed and will be replaced by new. It is hoped that by the end of this month all the major reconstruction work on the flight will have been completed. It had been planned that all of the lock gates for the flight would have been delivered and installed by the same date but unfortunately because of delays in delivery of the new gates—largely due to annual holidays at the factory concerned—it seems likely that at least 3 gates will still be required in October. These will probably be the bottom gates of Locks 41, 45 and 46. Mr. & Mrs. Knight, the volunteer lock gate fitters, have been at work almost every weekend fitting new gates and paddles and installing new sills. A quantity of B.C.N. bottom gate paddle gear has been obtained and also some from the abandoned Welshpool Arm and this is being installed throughout the flight. Work has been completed on Lock 54, almost completed on 55 and has started on Locks 52 and 53.

DREDGING. The canal has now been dredged to One Elm Bridge. [By Lock 52 in Stratford, where the A34 Birmingham Road crosses the canal. It was presumably so called from the proximity of the old elm marking the town boundary, which grew at the junction of Clopton Lane and the Birmingham Road.] Dredging is now progressing between One Elm Bridge and Lock 53 at Maidenhead Road. This is a particularly difficult section as the canal here is in a very steep cutting with only a narrow towing path. Fortunately, men from Western Command Plant Troop R.E. have, by the use of a small bulldozer, cut a 'road' into the canal bank from the main road level to the towing path and the Trust's Priestman Cub drag-line is dredging the pound from this 'road'. The mud in the canal here is probably deeper than at any other point, i.e. about 4′6″ [1.37m] to 4′ 9″ [1.44m] because of the great quantity of road silt which has been poured into the canal from the A34. The mud and debris beneath the Birmingham Road Bridge and the other bridges in Stratford will have to be removed by hand, i.e. shovelled into a skip which will then dump it on the canal bank or drop it into lorries. When this short section is dredged the only section remaining to be dealt with will be the last pound, i.e. that section between Locks 55 and 56—the barge lock into the river: this section includes the canal basin.

THE IMMEDIATE FUTURE. By the middle of November, work still to be done should include the reconstruction of Locks 52 and 53, the widening of Canada Bridge [Wilmcote], Spa Bridge [Bishopton] the railway bridge adjacent to Stratford Gas Works, and the clearing of the winding hole immediately north of Lock 39. When these tasks are completed the work parties will move back to the northern end of the canal in order to improve upon the work done at that end and carry out maintenance work. These operations will continue at least until the official opening in July 1964.

Appeals for volunteers have been virtually ignored by—even particularly by—those people and organisations most likely to benefit from the opening of the canal and it should be clearly understood that in spite of the progress made over the last few months, e.g. an average of 2 weeks to restore each of the locks on the Wilmcote Flight, there is no reason whatsoever for complacency. Help will be most urgently required *throughout* the winter months.

If you want a rally in Stratford in 1964 then P.Y.F's O. NOW!

Report by David Hutchings on Progress to early January 1964
LOCKS. Work is now completed on Lock 55 [Warwick Road, Stratford]. This lock, which has the greatest fall of any on the canal, contained far more mud than any other. Even after dredging by a grab the mud was still more than five feet [1.5 metres] deep and it had to be removed by hand with the aid of a small hoist. Work is also virtually completed on Lock 53 [Maidenhead Road]. The weir of this lock had, some years ago, become completely choked and instead of the stoppage being cleared the weir had been diverted into the chamber, thus making the lock inoperable. In addition, both of the gates and all of the paddles were useless and the lock was half-full of mud. The weir, which is underground for its entire length of about 100 feet [30 metres] has now been cleared and restored to its original form. Work is almost completed on Lock 52 [Birmingham Road] where about one-third of each wall has had to be rebuilt. The bottom gate of this lock should be delivered on Jan 9th. This gate will be the 70th and last in the programme, only five of the original lock gates having been retained. [The top ones at 21, 22, 26 and 38 and the bottom one at 24: all of these have since been replaced. There is an apparent discrepancy of one gate, in that 70 were replaced and 5 retained: the extra one replaced was a flood gate at Bridge 57, immediately to the south of Edstone Aqueduct.] Thus apart from the fitting of the bottom gates of Locks 45, 46 and 47 which are in position on the Wilmcote Flight, and the bottom gate of

Lock 51, the lock restoration programme will have been completed, although the top gate of Lock 52 will have to be refitted.

This does not mean that no work remains to be done. Many of the locks which were restored in the early part of the programme have now to be checked over, repointing is required in many cases after the ravages of last winter's frost, side weirs will require repairs. It is planned to remove all of the original Stratford canal bottom gate paddle gear and replace it with B.C.N. or S.U.C. type. At present, 21 of the 36 locks on the canal are equipped with this excellent gear.

DREDGING. During the last month the drag-line has been engaged in further dredging of Pounds 55/56, 53/54 and the clearing of Lock 53. It is intended that further improvement work will be carried out in Stratford and that the drag-line will then be moved to Bishopton where about 50 yards [46 metres] of canal have yet to be dredged.

GENERAL. Considerable difficulty has been caused by recent acts of hooliganism on the canal and on three occasions Pound 38/39 [about 3 miles (4.8km) long, from Preston Bagot nearly to Edstone Aqueduct] has been drained and thus Pound 39/40 [another 3 miles (4.8km) to the top of Wilmcote] has fallen whilst the pound above it refilled. Major bank repairs comprising the installation of a five feet [1.5 metres] deep reinforced concrete wall have been carried out on Pound 39/40. These pounds have now been refilled and thus the canal is navigable to the head of Lock 45, i.e. approximately half-way down the Wilmcote Flight. When the lock gates mentioned above are fitted and the short undredged section at Bishopton has been cleared a boat will be able to enter Stratford. However, it will not be possible for a full-width boat to make use of some of the Wilmcote locks until some of the iron bumpers which were left protruding when the lock walls were rebuilt have been cut off. Up to the present no satisfactory way of doing this work has been found. [It was eventually done in May, by the Calor firm at no charge, using an oxygen/Calor gas/iron powder flame cutting process.]

The response to appeals for volunteers has been unsatisfactory of late, except that the remarkable Mr. & Mrs. Knight have together fitted most of the lock gates on the canal. Fortunately the weather has been fairly good and the parties of prisoners from Winson Green Gaol have been able to make fair progress.

Expenditure to November 1963 was £44,600, leaving about £3,500 still available. To this can be added an estimated income of £1,500 for 1964.

At 3.45pm on 22 February 1964 the first boat, *Laughing Water II* owned by Mr J. D. Tompkins of Stratford, reached the Avon at Stratford via the restored canal. It was only a small launch, full-width narrow boats still being prevented from passing the Wilmcote Flight by the protruding iron rubbing bars mentioned in the canal manager's report. Although the passage of this launch heralded the completion of restoration, in practice there was still a great deal to be done.

Many problems had to be solved with regard to 'Timothy's Bridge', No 64, on the outskirts of Stratford. This was to be rebuilt, not as part of the restoration, but to a higher traffic standard to give improved access to a new industrial estate then being built. It would have been necessary, however, to rebuild it anyway, since this was the bridge noted at the start of restoration as being in urgent need of repairs and being progressively demolished by children. Messrs Industrial Design and Construction Ltd, the builders of the new estate, were given specifications and conditions for the temporary Bailey bridge they wished to erect. These included the proviso that the cast-iron parts of the original bridge were to be preserved since it was one of the split ones. It is not known whether they were preserved and, if so, where they are now. The Bailey bridge appeared suddenly, late in 1963, without either the agreement of the National Trust and its Restoration Committee, or prior knowledge that its construction was imminent. As originally erected, this temporary bridge was only a few feet above the water line and the constructors had to be persuaded to raise it, which was done a few weeks later. The raising proved necessary, for the temporary bridge was still there when the canal was officially reopened.

This however, was the least part of the problem. Formal plans drawn up by the council for the permanent bridge, which first came to the notice of the Local Restoration Committee in February 1964, incorporated a headroom of only 6ft 6in (1.98m) above the water line. This had been agreed by the National Trust to the council in 1961, but a statutory minimum of 6ft 9in (2m) was laid down by the 1793 act of parliament which authorised the canal. There was also a problem over the clearance between the bridge abutments, the original having been an accommodation bridge with the towpath passing over it while its replacement was to be a road bridge under which the towpath would have to pass.

The Local Restoration Committee was 'strongly of the opinion' that the headroom should be 8ft (2.4m) together with 8ft (2.4m) clearance on each side of the channel between it and the bridge abutments. Stratford council responded by offering 7ft (2.1m) headroom and pointed out that if the height was increased further, the sight line of approaching traffic would be impaired. The Trust urged that this be accepted. The Local Restoration Committee eventually decided that it would agree to 7ft 3in (2.2m) measured above water level at weir height, provided that first, the foundations of the bridge abutments were not less than 20ft (6m) apart and allowed a towpath of not less than 5ft (1.5m) beside the existing channel, and second, the bridge was so sited that there was a clear 70ft (21.3m) of deep water, measured in a straight line at right angles to the bridge, on either side of it. In April 1964 the Borough Council agreed to these terms.

Another major trouble-spot still needing attention before the canal could be properly reopened was Lock 30 at Lowsonford. Since the time when narrow boats had been able to get down the restored canal to this point it had been known that there were two problems. The first was that some boats had difficulty entering the lock because of the inward movement of the walls (the same trouble as had been found in the locks of the Wilmcote Flight). The second problem was that all boats with a cabin superstructure had difficulty in getting through the bridge at the tail of the lock. This may have been caused by a design fault in the original construction, the bridge being slightly out of line with the lock as well as very low and narrow. The combination of these factors caused many boats to catch their cabins on the bridge, or even jam under it. In order to correct these defects the nearside wall of the lock had to be demolished and rebuilt about 15in (38cm) further back, starting from a point just inside the heel of the top gate, so that the lock chamber is now over 8ft (2.4m) wide rather than its original 7ft (2.1m) or so and the bottom gate is offset. However, the gate and the clearance through it retains the original dimensions. As well as giving extra clearance within the lock, this alteration enables boats to realign for the bridge as they leave the lock. Unlike most of the other rebuilt lock walls, this one had to be demolished right down to the foundations and the demolition had to extend right through the bridge to include the towpath approach wall. In addition, in order to offset the bottom gate, the mitre-post on the opposite wall, to which the far end of the gate closes, was moved inwards.

Because of all the other work still proceeding on other parts of the canal, it was not possible to start this extra work at Lock 30 until the end of April 1964 and it was still not finished when the first boats heading for the reopening rally arrived at the lock at midday on Sunday 28 June. Several of their crew members joined the prisoners working on the lock and the last structural concrete was poured as darkness fell on Tuesday evening. After allowing time for this to cure, the boats passed through on the evening of Thursday 2 July—only nine days before the opening ceremony.

As water levels were brought up during the early part of 1964, encouraged by putting boards on some weirs, leaks began to appear and claimed much attention. In January a large leak above Canada Bridge at Wilmcote and two others at Lowsonford were found and mended. By February, two men were permanently employed on leak sealing and the weirs at Locks 31 (Lowsonford) and 39 (the Odd Lock) had each to be lowered by 3in (7cm) to prevent overflowing of parts of the bank that were not high enough. In March it was decided that Edstone Aqueduct would have to be emptied in order to repair the seals between the ends of the iron trough and the brick abutments, which was done by injecting a mastic-type material. Leaks were also attended in the walls of the basin at Wootton Wawen.

Potentially more seriously, part of the bank supporting the southern abutment of Wootton Wawen Aqueduct and the offside embankment of the canal was removed around March or April by the County Council in the course of a road-widening scheme. This started leaks and caused a crack to appear in the brickwork of the abutment. After 'vigorous action' (words as minuted) by David Hutchings, the County Council agreed to be responsible for any circumstances arising and to make repairs to the satisfaction of the Restoration Committee. These were completed in May.

At the April meeting of the committee a toll of £1 2s 6d was agreed for all powered craft for one week and pro rata for up to four weeks. Longer term and residential licence rates were also fixed, the maximum being £24 for a powered boat over 50ft (15m) for one year.

The remainder of the restoration period developed into a race against time, with hundreds of minor but important matters and some major ones still to be dealt with. Mindful of possible deficiencies still existing, the Restoration Committee made an inspection cruise of the lower end of the canal on 31 May. This once again involved *Emscote* and also *Linda*, which was being worked down from Wootton Wawen to Stratford for a rehearsal of the Queen Mother's opening cruise. *Emscote* had been brought down to the Stratford side of Lock 30 before it was closed at the end of April for the rebuilding already described. A date for the inspection cruise had proved difficult to arrange because pipe laying was taking place in the bed of the canal in Stratford (having been agreed in advance of the restoration by BTW) and there was no water at all beyond the bottom of Wilmcote Flight. The inspection cruise was not without its problems and at the June meeting of the committee, which was the last before the reopening rally, it was minuted that: 'The canal is not as readily navigable as might be expected—persons intending to bring boats to the rally should be warned that they may encounter some difficulties.'

Mr King, the Vice-Chairman of the Local Restoration Committee, wrote to the National Trust as follows:

Resulting from the test voyage in *Emscote*. I have been particularly worried for a long time about the management of the canal after it has been reopened.

I really do feel very strongly that the Trust should make a decision at the earliest possible moment as to what is to happen. David is organising the rally, as I believe you know. This in itself is a mammoth job. He just has not the time to do everything and I do feel that the Trust should endeavour to get someone to help him with the actual management of the canal. As you know, I have no technical knowledge of the canal but it was obvious even to me last weekend that there is going to be a serious shortage of water for 150 boats to come down the canal to Stratford for the rally. When I tell you that it took some six hours to pass *Emscote* from Wilmcote Bridge down to Bishopton (less than 2 miles [3.2km] and 11 locks) you will see that although *Linda* eventually got through to Stratford the time taken was not inconsiderable. One of the difficulties appeared to be shortage of water. Enthusiasm, idealism and optimism, however, are not going to be enough to cope with the Rally of Boats and I do earnestly ask that someone with knowledge of canals should spend anything up to a week on the practical side of seeing that the rally can in fact take place without too much discomfort for those taking part.

Specifically, the Local Restoration Committee noted that in order to make a successful rally possible, the following required immediate attention: a) completion of work on Lock 30; b) improvement in water levels; c) removal of ledge in Lock 49 (though as a temporary measure it was possibly more expedient to raise the water in the pound below by means of a board on the weir).

It would undoubtedly have been preferable not to work to

such a tight deadline but the canal had to be opened to traffic so that the National Trust could obtain usage and income figures to assist in their consideration of whether to take it over when their temporary lease expired in September 1965. Furthermore, the Inland Waterways Association had arranged a reopening rally in the presence of Her Majesty the Queen Mother. (The Restoration Committee were not consulted about the rally arrangements; indeed, not long before the event they inquired whether they were to receive tickets to attend the ceremonies.) So the die was cast: the Queen Mother was coming on 11 July 1964.

13
Canal Cottages

The account of the restoration must be completed by mention of the canal cottages. Originally, there were twelve lengthsmen's cottages on the southern section of the Stratford Canal, situated by each of the following locks: 22 Kingswood; 25 Dick's Lane; 28 north of Lowsonford; 31 Lowsonford; 34 Yarningale; 37 Preston Bagot; 39 Odd Lock, Bearley; 40, 44 and 50 Wilmcote Flight; 51 Bishopton; and 54 Stratford.

Of these, the six from Locks 22–37 inclusive are of the barrel-roofed type which is unique to the southern Stratford Canal; furthermore, they occur only in the section from Kingswood to Wootton Wawen, built during 1812 and 1813 by William James. The roof of this type is formed of a semi-circular brick arch such as is used for tunnels and some bridges and the parallel main walls are tied together by iron rods to take the sideways thrust of the weight of this arch. The remainder of the cottages, from Wootton Wawen to Stratford, are or were of the conventional pitched-roof type. In addition to the lengthsmen's cottages there was also a small 'manager's house' near Lock 21 at Kingswood.

The two cottages which still exist alongside the towpath just north of Featherbed Lane Bridge at Wilmcote were not for lengthsmen but were part of the complex that once existed there to serve the transhipment wharves for stone brought by tramway from the quarries near Wilmcote. They may have been built and owned by the quarry company. In any event, they were not part of the canal estate at the time of the take-over of the canal by the National Trust in 1960.

By the time of that take-over, the barrel-roofed cottages at

Locks 25, 34 and 37 had already been sold and were in private ownership and the pitched-roofed ones at Locks 39, 50 and 51 had been demolished or had fallen down. The one at Lock 51 had already gone in 1956 when the Stratford-on-Avon Canal Society was formed. That at Lock 39 was a ruin in 1956 and disappeared shortly after. The one at Lock 50 remained occupied until 1956, but by 1957 it was unoccupied and beginning to crumble under the attention of vandals, and by 1959 it, too, was only a pile of rubble.

Thus, the National Trust took over the house at Lock 21; three barrel-roofed cottages at Locks 22, 28 and 31; and three pitched-roofed ones at Locks 40, 44 and 54. In June 1959 the Trust's area agent had reported on their condition as follows:

No 1 [Lock 21] Lapworth. In a state of extreme disrepair internally with plaster off many of the walls and ceilings. It has electricity and well water but no sanitation. Mains water is available. Estimated costs: repairs £900, improvements £800.

No 2 [Lock 22] Lapworth. Has electricity and well water. No sanitation. Repairs £400, improvements £850.

No 3 [Lock 28] Lowsonford. Water from a well of unknown quality. No electricity. Structurally reasonable. Repairs £200, no improvements envisaged.

No 4 [Lock 31] Lowsonford. Mains water and electricity are available nearby but not connected. Repairs £250, improvement £1,200.

No 5 [Lock 40] Wilmcote. Very damp. On council special list. No electricity. Water from a shallow well. I cannot recommend acceptance of this cottage. If accepted I can only recommend demolition.

No 6 [Lock 44] Wilmcote. Damp. Also on council special list. No electricity, water from a shallow well. The council might well put a closing order on it. I cannot recommend acceptance. If accepted, I recommend demolition.

No 7 [Lock 54] Stratford. Poor construction, no charm. Very damp and dark. Extremely bad repair. No electricity, water from a well. Council have put it on their list for demolition. I consider it would be more satisfactory to demolish and build afresh. I cannot recommend acceptance. If accepted, I recommend demolition.

Other records suggest that had the take-over by the National Trust not occurred, the British Transport Commission planned to retain only two of them, although which two is not recorded.

The cottages at Locks 21 and 54 were occupied, respectively, by Mr Gilbert and Mr Hancox, the two ex-BTW lengthsmen who continued in employment with the National Trust. That at Lock 31 was rented by a non-employee, Mrs Taylor, a sitting tenant inherited from BTW. All three continued in the same occupation throughout and indeed beyond the restoration period, the stability of their tenure probably being associated with their reasonable access. The barrel-roofed cottage at Lock 22, which also has reasonable access, was already vacant in 1960 before the Trust took over and became occupied by Mr Hutchings after he was appointed Restoration Manager.

The other three cottages, at Locks 28, 40 and 44, were another matter altogether. They are the most difficult of access, being approachable only by a long journey along the towpath or, in the case of that at Lock 40, by a right of way across fields. By the summer of 1960 the one at Lock 40 had become empty and the existing tenant of the one at Lock 44 moved to that at Lock 40. The now empty one at Lock 44 immediately attracted the attention of vandals and the Canal Society did what it could to prevent damage by boarding up windows and visiting the cottage as often as possible. The Stratford-on-Avon Rural District Council then announced that it proposed to make a 'closing order' on it on the grounds that it was unfit for human habitation. A statutory alternative to such an order was for the owners of the cottage to undertake not to use it for human habitation until it had been put in order. This the National Trust was prepared to do, but could not legally do so until after the cottage had been transferred to it, with the canal, in September. The District Council was persuaded to leave the matter in abeyance until then.

As has already been noted, on take-over the cottages became the responsibility of the Regional Secretary of the National Trust, Sir Dawson Bates, working via the Local Restoration Committee. The Trust decided that because all the money likely to be raised would be needed for restoration of the waterway itself, it was not feasible for the time being to bring any of the cottages up to the Trust's normally high standard. Instead, the Restoration Committee was asked to obtain estimates for the minimum work to conform with the requirements of the local authorities. Mr Burton undertook this task and his first concern was the cottage at Lock 44. It transpired that most of the work required was arrears of maintenance together with cleaning of the polluted well, this being the only source of water. The RDC was satisfied with the sanitary arrangements and would not insist on the provision of a bathroom. The estimate was £665 (a considerable sum in those days) and it was decided to advertise the cottage rent-free for five years to someone prepared to do repairs to a value of £500 within six months. A Mr Sanders and his family became the nominal tenants of this cottage at the end of 1960, though under the terms of the undertaking which the National Trust had now given he could not occupy it until the work was done. The tenancy agreement also required Mr Sanders to render twenty-four hours service to the canal restoration each month. There was a further tenant during 1965 and 1966 followed by a period during which it stood empty and was again vandalised. It was repaired again by two young men and finally, during the 1970s, was sold into private ownership.

By the end of 1960 the Stratford-upon-Avon Borough Council had stated that it proposed to serve notice that the cottage at Lock 54, occupied by Mr Hancox, was below standard. Mr Burton was again asked to obtain estimates for the minimum work necessary, but this course of action became diverted in the spring of 1961 because the owners of adjacent land were discussing an exchange with the National

Trust. This would provide the adjacent owners with better access to their site and the Trust with a new cottage. Such an exchange had to be agreed by the British Transport Commission since the Trust's lease at the time was for five years only. In the autumn of 1961 it was believed that the BTC had agreed in principle, but for some unrecorded reason the exchange never happened. By the spring of 1962 the Borough Council was again pressing the matter and was reminded that the building of a new cottage was still under discussion and that it would need planning permission. Permission was obtained in September for the building of a new cottage on the old site, but this never took place. Following the death of Mr Hancox the old cottage was finally demolished in 1976 on behalf of the council, and the site is now empty.

Further problems began in May 1961 over the cottage at Lock 40. The previous tenant had left and the cottage had been damaged by vandals, but Stratford RDC agreed to immediate reoccupation provided that certain repair work was done, at an estimated cost of £368. By July of that year the cottage was occupied by Mr Berry, who had already started some of the work—the RDC specified that it must be completed within six months from the date of occupation. Because Mr Berry spent long hours on canal restoration work it was necessary to give him specific time off, during wet weather, to work on the cottage. The work was substantially completed by June 1963 and a very good job was made of it. Although Mr Berry himself left at the end of the canal restoration period, the cottage is still occupied on tenancy from the National Trust.

The final cottage to cause problems was that at Lock 28. In August 1961 the previous tenant announced his intention of leaving and the cottage, which was completely without services and in poor order, was offered to Mr French who was also employed in canal restoration work. However, the previous tenant did not leave for some time and by 1963 a demolition order had been placed on it by Warwick Rural

District Council, subject to withdrawal if the necessary work was done. In June 1963 the cottage was offered to a Mr Tullett, who wanted a ten-year lease in exchange for his undertaking repairs to an estimated value of £750 and acting as 'voluntary' lengthsman between Locks 26 and 30. Since the National Trust's lease of the canal only ran to September 1965, twenty-seven months was the longest lease that could legally be offered on the cottage 'with hopeful assurances for the future'. Mr Tullett worked on the cottage during the latter part of 1963 but left in January 1964, when the tenancy passed to a Mr Perry who submitted new plans for modernisation. The work was done, the demolition order lifted, and this cottage also remains occupied on tenancy from the National Trust.

Thus it can be seen that some of the cottages had a very chequered history. However, except for that at Lock 54 all those taken over by the National Trust have survived and five of them are still in the possession of the Trust, including three of the six unique barrel-roofed ones.

14
Reopening

The Inland Waterways Association's 1964 Annual Boat Rally formed the basis of the festivities organised to mark the reopening to navigation of the restored southern section of the Stratford-upon-Avon Canal and for that occasion was re-christened 'The National Festival of Boats and Arts'. About 200 boats entered for the rally, which was from 9 to 14 July, with the actual reopening ceremony on Saturday 11 July.

Since the Upper Avon, from Evesham to Stratford, was not then open (its restoration only began some years later), all these boats had to come down the canal and in the main they did so during the week before the rally. The very success of the rally in attracting large numbers of boats was nearly its undoing for it is unlikely that the canal had ever experienced such intensity of traffic, even in its commercial heyday. It had always had water supply problems, from the time when it was first built, and restoration had done nothing to alleviate these. In anticipation of possible difficulties and to ease the passage of the boats, voluntary lengthsmen/lock-keepers were on duty at several points and the army provided radio communication between the canal staff and their office.

As expected, some difficulties occurred. Because of the 'bunching' of boats, which always occurs when slower boats are among many, and the fact that they were all going in the same direction, water levels in some of the pounds went up and down alarmingly. When they were excessively up water ran away to waste and when they were down the deeper-draught boats became stuck. Releasing them meant either letting water down from above, thus robbing higher pounds, or waiting until the arrival of further boats which brought some more water with them but increased the bunching effect. A few boat crews found it too much of a strain and some tempers flared. One lady, having heaved unsuccessfully on the end of a shaft from a 70ft (21m) narrow boat for quite some time, exclaimed 'Let's go and find that Hutchings and throw him in his own canal!'—a most unfair and completely undeserved fate for one who had given and achieved so much, but those who have been in predicaments on boats may perhaps forgive her such thoughts in the heat of the moment.

There were teething troubles with some of the lock mechanisms which led to minor stoppages while temporary repairs were made, and one stoppage of twenty-four hours owing to a paddle failure at Lock 38 for which no spare was immediately available. Some of the preserved working boats were found to be a very tight fit in some of the locks for, while most locks on the canal system in general are rather wider than their nominal dimensions, some of the Stratford Canal locks were (and still are) an exact 7ft 1in (2.16m). Although this should be sufficient for any boat of narrow-beam standard, old boats have sometimes spread or twisted to a slight banana-shape. Lock 44 on the Wilmcote Flight proved particularly troublesome for such boats and it became necessary to winch some of them into this lock on their return journey from the rally. A few decided that discretion was the better part of valour and did not go down to Stratford, but instead staged their own mini-rally at Wootton Wawen. No great trouble was experienced with the ledge in Lock 49 once the water level had been raised in the pound below by putting planks on the weir.

The vast majority of boats got through without any more difficulty than is always experienced when large numbers of boats are all going the same way at the same time and the river at Stratford was filled with the (for then) vast assembly of boats and their thousand or so crew members. There were also thousands of visitors, attracted by the boats and the restoration exhibition on the rally site, the Avon Bank

Riverside Gardens, kindly lent for the purpose by the Trustees of the Royal Shakespeare Memorial Theatre.

On the opening day itself, the principal guests embarked at 3.30pm on the *Lady Hatherton* and *Arcturus*, and Her Majesty Queen Elizabeth the Queen Mother and the very important guests on *Linda* at Tyler Street Wharf (which is at the back of the council's dustcart yard). This flotilla proceeded down the last two narrow locks, Nos 54 and 55, led by the narrow boat *Danube*. It is said that in one of the locks, a stream of water emerging from a hole in the wall in direct line with the Queen Mother, threatened to soak her as the boat descended. The day was saved by the Earl of Crawford and Balcarres, KT, GBE, Chairman of the National Trust, who put his thumb over the hole and diverted the water. On reaching the Bancroft Basin, the escorting boats paused while *Linda* entered the final barge lock which leads out into the river. Here the Earl of Crawford made a short speech welcoming the Queen Mother, who replied and cut a tape stretched across the lock, to formally open the canal. The boats then proceeded on to the Avon to the site of the Inland Waterways Association's exhibition 'The National Festival of Boats and Arts' where the Queen Mother was received by Mr M. J. MacFarlane, council member of the IWA. The royal visitor left the exhibition at 5.15, but all was by no means over since in the evening there was a special performance of *Henry V* in the theatre, which the Queen Mother attended. After supper on the theatre balconies there was a performance of *Water Music*, specially composed for the occasion by Malcolm Arnold, followed by Handel's *Fireworks Music* accompanied by fireworks, the music being performed from a raft moored in the river. Financial help to stage these festivities came from Shell-BP and physical help from the Royal Engineers.

The southern section of the Stratford-upon-Avon Canal was open again after being unnavigable, or virtually so, for around forty years. This table, from the rally brochure, shows what the restoration involved:

The Canal

Length	About 13 miles [21km]
Number of locks	36
Number of lock paddles	112
Number of aqueducts	3
Number of bridges	69[1]
Number of days to 'complete' restoration (ie first boat through to River Avon from Lapworth)	1,058 days

Money

Cost of abandonment—about	£10,000 per mile [1.6km]
Cost of abandonment and effectively filling in—about	£70,000 per mile [1.6km]
Cost of restoration by 'normal' means—about	£7,500 per mile [1.6km]
Cost of restoration by National Trust, not using 'normal' means—about	£3,500 per mile [1.6km][2]

Things

Amount of muck dredged from canal—about	200,000cu yd [150,000cu m]
Maximum rate of dredging	2½ miles [4km] per month
Number of locks requiring major repairs or rebuilding	30
Average time to demolish and virtually rebuild a lock (Wilmcote Flight)	16 days

[1] Incorrect in the brochure, being the number on the whole Stratford Canal. Only twenty-three are on the southern section.

[2] The National Trust's estimate for the final total cost of restoration was £61,233, which amounts to £4,500 per mile (1.6km). The discrepancy between this and the figure in the rally brochure is probably mainly due to the inclusion of salaries by the Trust. Towards this expenditure, £53,000 had been received (£33,000 donations, £20,000 ministry grant) and some £8,000 had been advanced from the Trust's general funds in anticipation of repayment from seven-year covenants.

Maximum amount of debris removed from demolished lock (same amount of new material taken in)—about	250 tons
Number of lock gates replaced by new	70—out of 75 (includes 1 stop gate)
Number of paddles replaced	112 out of 112
Maximum rate of removing old lock gates	18 in two days
Maximum rate of producing and installing new gates	4 in ten days
Maximum rate of gate fitting	3 in two days

Individual donors who had contributed £500 or more were invited to accept commemoration by having their names displayed on cast-iron plaques mounted by the sides of individual locks. Not all wished to do so but the following locks were so dedicated:

33 Mr Gordon Gray Trust
41 Cadbury Trust
42 Trustee of Lady Hind, deceased
45 Francis C. Scott Trust
46 H. E. M. Benn
47 Miss Farewell Jones
48 Eleanor Rathbone Trust
49 John Feeney Charitable Trust
50 Pilgrim Trust
55 Douglas King

Sadly, it was not anticipated that these plaques would prove attractive to vandals; the mountings were not vandal-proof and most have now disappeared. The same fate has overtaken many of the National Trust plaques mounted on the lock beams.

More than just money and things, the restoration had involved people and one person in particular. It was perhaps best summed up by an article in the *Sunday Times* which read: 'They said it couldn't be done, but David did it. They said the obstacles were impossible, but David just crawled over them. He flattened them as he went.' But to do it he had worked fourteen or more hours a day, seven days a week, for three years. In an interview he said:

People say we have left our mark on the map of England. I suppose we have. But there was nothing heroic about it. It was a sordid, filthy, hefting, digging, canting, back-breaking, heart-breaking, never-ending job, all mud and water and slime. If I had known what it would be like before I started, I don't think I could have done it. When the National Trust asked me to do it we had no plans, no tools, no men, no money, no anything. Ever since, it's been a job of getting contacts, persuading them to help, scrounging equipment, making people give things they didn't want to give, volunteer when they didn't want to and work far harder than they wanted to for much longer than they wanted. Once you cut a bit of red tape, you find an Aladdin's Cave of money and facilities. If you go in high enough, you can get any organisation to do anything. And if they say no, just try again higher up until they say 'yes'. We have proved it can be done, that everything needed can be got if you try.

In the rally brochure, he wrote:

Those who were to do the job had nothing and knew nothing but they began with one overwhelming advantage, they were not Experts and therefore did not know what could not be done.

As a result of his work on the canal, David Hutchings received an MBE in the New Year's Honours list for 1965.

15
The Trust Takes the Freehold

The National Trust's five-year lease on the canal was due to expire on 28 September 1965. There was then an option: either for the Trust to terminate its association with the canal, letting it revert to the British Waterways Board, or to have the freehold of the canal permanently vested in the Trust at no charge. Notice of choice of option was required six months in advance of the expiry of the lease, namely, by 25 March 1965, only ten months after the reopening.

The outcome was by no means certain because it was becoming apparent to the Trust that the canal might not be self-supporting and one of the stated conditions on which they had accepted it initially was that they should incur no financial liability. To help with the considerations they commissioned two reports, one from David Hutchings and one independently from the Laing Construction Company Limited. No copy of the latter has come to light, although the salient features of it can be gleaned from other documents. It is thus worth reproducing parts of Mr Hutchings' report in some detail.

Summary of the present situation and proposals for the future use, maintenance, improvement, development, financing and staffing of the Stratford-on-Avon Canal (southern section).

Summary of present situation
1   Administration and staffing.
The administration comprises the Canal Manager and his Secretary based at the Canal Depot in Lapworth. Much of the Manager's time is spent on and about the canal organising and supervising working

parties, carrying out inspections, visiting riparian owners, etc. The permanent labour force comprises two men.

2   Physical state of the waterway.

2a   The pounds. Dredging. Except for the upper half of Pound 21/22 [Lapworth]—a distance of about 50 yards [45 metres]—all parts of the canal have been dredged at least once and some of the more difficult sections two or three times. Most of the pounds will pass boats of up to 3ft 6ins [1.06m] draught <u>provided the water level is at its full height</u> [his underlining]. Certain sections, particularly where large drains or ditches feed into the canal, will require periodic redredging.

Banks. The banks are generally in poor condition, due to a number of factors. These include the nature of the original construction, neglect of maintenance work over the last 100 years, because rodents and tree roots have pierced the banks in many places, because of the effect of weather and water erosion and because there is virtually no piling or other form of bank protection on the waterway. Heavy use of the canal by motorised boats will worsen the situation. Some of the embankments are prone to serious leakage and the majority of the time of the permanent staff is at present spent dealing with this.

2b   The locks. Gates. All but five have been replaced and these five appear to be fit for some years' service except for the bottom gate of Lock 24 which should either be thoroughly repaired or replaced as soon as is convenient.

Sills. In most cases the gate clap sills have been replaced and where this has not been done, new oak sill liners have been fitted. No new main sills have been required.

Paddles and gear. Virtually all of the lock paddles have been replaced, as has much of the paddle gear.

Chambers. All have been dredged at least once and some two or three times. Repairs have ranged from repointing and patching to complete rebuilding.

Bypass weirs. Extensive repairs have been carried out to many and in some cases their levels have been adjusted, either up or down. Weirs at Locks 26 to 29 remain to be finally repaired but although these weirs leak there is little loss of water from the canal. All the side weirs run for much of their length underground and wherever possible and when convenient they should be brought to surface level and debris baffles erected to prevent choking, as has been done at Lock 22.

2c   Other structures. Aqueducts. All three are in fairly good condition and long-standing leaks have been dealt with on the Edstone [Bearley] and Wootton Wawen Aqueducts.

Flood paddles have been overhauled and if necessary replaced. The flood paddle which was situated on the offside of the canal immediately north of Bridge 57 [south of Bearley Aqueduct] has been replaced by a complete new paddle and chamber on the opposite bank.

Bridges. The road bridges on the canal are at present the responsibility of either the Ministry of Transport, the Local Authority, or British Waterways Board. It is understood that, when the final take-over takes place, the latter will become the responsibility of the Trust and this is being looked into by the Trust's Legal Department. The accommodation bridges are generally in good condition, although a programme of minor repairs and improvements is planned.

3   Maintenance.

3a   The pounds. Maintenance work will have to be carried out constantly to keep the waterway in a navigable condition. Required work includes the redredging of resilted sections in both the locks and the pounds; the sealing of constantly recurring leaks; the strengthening and protecting of the vulnerable embankments, possibly by piling or walling; the removal or cutting back of the canal side trees; dealing with any extensive water weed growth; levelling and mowing of the towing path; laying of the boundary hedges and repairs to boundary fences, etc.

3b   The locks. It will be necessary periodically to repoint sections of the chambers and approach walls, to carry out refitting of the lock gates and paddles, to lubricate and adjust the paddle gear and to paint or tar the gates and paddle starts. It is recommended that wherever possible the locks are kept full so that both of the gates are kept wet. The bottom gates on the locks are of the single type whereas more usually bottom gates are in pairs and are mitred. This latter arrangement is the more desirable for a number of reasons, one of the most important being that the gate structure is thus much stronger and is far more able to resist being struck by the prow of a boat than is the single gate structure. A great strain is put on the bottom gates on this canal when they are struck by, for example, a 15 ton narrow boat moving at 3 or 4 miles [4.8 or 6.4 kilometres] per hour, particularly if the boat is not fitted with front fenders. The area of impact is only 2 inches [50 centimetres] and it occurs at the weakest point on the balance beam.

3c Other structures. Bridges and aqueducts. Repointing and the cutting out and replacement of eroded brickwork, painting or tarring of the metal portions and the sealing of any leaks which may occur from the aqueducts, will be required from time to time.

4 Improvements. Many improvements are desirable and if carried out would probably lead to increased use of the waterway which in turn should lead to increased revenue. Possible improvements include:

a Minor work to certain lock chambers so that wider boats may pass through; although any boat with a beam of more than 6′ 10″ [2m] has no redress, this being the statutory beam for the waterway. Boats of up to 7′ 3″ [2.2m] have passed through, with some difficulties, but an 'official' nominal gauge of 7′ 1″ [2.1m] is suggested.
b The provision of equipped moorings at Lapworth, Dick's Lane, Lowsonford, Preston Bagot, Wootton Wawen, Wilmcote, and Stratford Pounds 53/54 and the upper half of Pound 55/56.
c Removal of sections of the towing path hedge to improve views.
d The provision of volunteer lock-keepers/lengthsmen.
e Provision of extra paddles so that locks may be worked more quickly.
f Provision of silt interceptor chambers at all places where ditches or road drains discharge into the canal.
g The clearing and levelling of the towing path.
h Improvement in the water supply and attention to constantly recurring leaks.

A number of possible developments are then listed, followed by financial estimates. The income for 1964 is estimated at £3,580 (which includes the annual sum of £1,500 from British Waterways, due to cease in 1965). Estimated future annual income is given as £4,020 and expenditure as £4,600, not including the cost of any improvements or developments and based on the following staffing:

1   A part-time Administrative Manager who would be based at the Canal Office at Lapworth. It has been suggested that this post might be combined with the Curatorship of Packwood House, a Trust property about two miles [3.2 kilometres] from the canal. He would also have a part-time Secretary.

2   An outside Manager or Foreman who would have charge of the prisoners and volunteer labour and would be largely responsible for any local technical decision on the waterway.

3a   Two full-time and one part-time lengthsmen/labourers.

3b   About 12 prisoners working under the control of a Prison Officer, himself under the control of the outside Manager.

3c   A number of volunteer lengthsmen/lock-keepers drawn from amongst the occupiers of the canal cottages and the owners of houseboats on the canal.

Mr Hutchings' report ends with an illuminating consideration of 'the use of volunteer and other unpaid labour'.

It appears to be widely thought that the use of volunteer or unpaid labour is a universal solution to all of the labour problems connected with projects which otherwise would not be carried out. Experience over the last $3\frac{1}{2}$ years has, however, indicated very forcibly that there are many difficulties involved and these should be carefully considered before arrangements for the employment of future labour are made. The problems are largely connected with supervision, the lack of experience and skill, and the character of the people concerned. Volunteers normally arrive full of enthusiasm but with little understanding of the nature and magnitude of the problems involved or of the conditions under which they are expected to work. At no time during the canal restoration operations have weather or near-impossible conditions been allowed to halt the work, but after a few hours of standing up to his waist in cold stinking mud at the bottom of a wind and rain lashed lock chamber with apparently no hope of his ever achieving the somewhat obscure aim of the operation, an even stout-hearted volunteer begins to wonder whether perhaps he has made a mistake, particularly as it is often not possible to make adequate arrangements for the drying of clothes and for hot baths. The work on the canal has always and inevitably been of a very heavy and sometimes dangerous nature and it is perhaps remarkable that no deaths or serious injuries have resulted.

It was found that volunteers arrived fairly willingly when the job first began and that many of them would return two or three times, but gradually the numbers dwindled until by the middle of the second year the volunteer parties were very small indeed and normally comprised only a few stout-hearted people such as Mr. and Mrs. Knight and other members of the IWA. Virtually no member of the Canal Society was tempted to offer his services, possibly because he was well aware of the conditions on the canal. Often the most willing volunteer had little or no skill, was quite unable at first to effectively use even the simplest tools and often had no knowledge whatever of materials or plant. Thus the valuable time of the skilled or semi-skilled supervisor was wasted whilst detailed explanations were given, whilst faulty work was replaced, or whilst maintenance work was carried out on machines which were damaged or at least brought to a halt because of well-meaning but incompetent handling by volunteers. Large quantities of tools and materials have been lost and broken through careless or unskilled handling, this particularly applies to perishable articles such as cement, paint, etc. The comparatively heavy expenditure on plant maintenance and replacement emphasises the problems mentioned above. It does not appear to be fully understood that no store of knowledge or experience can necessarily be built up as the labour force is constantly changing, an hour spent training volunteers in how to carry out a simple operation is completely lost if those volunteers do not return on another occasion and the whole procedure has to be repeated for a newly arriving party which in its turn may never come again. It has been virtually impossible to maintain adequate control over the issue and use of tools and although on many occasions it has been known which volunteer damaged or lost the item, it has nevertheless been impossible to demand any restitution. One cannot sack a volunteer nor fine him, he is quite free to walk off the job whenever he feels inclined and only the force of character of the supervisor is available to see that he does not.

Prison labour is equally vulnerable, but with certain differences. For example, it is an advantage that most of the prisoners want to be outside the prison but on the other hand they do not want to work and without supervision they normally do not. Again only forceful supervision—and the threat of being sent back inside—will keep them working. Certain prisoners undoubtedly arrive with the intention of doing as little work as possible and of obtaining the maximum of unofficial 'comforts', and this latter intention probably accounts for the fact that large quantities of tools, particularly of the smaller variety, have been lost by the prison working parties. In only one case did the Prison Officer in charge of the working party manage to keep all the tools. This Officer was an ex-R.S.M. and forcefully insisted on a tool check night and morning.

Although these and many other problems occur it seems certain that the use of unpaid labour is the only practical solution to the labour problems presented by projects such as the canal restoration, but undoubtedly the key to the whole matter is the provision of adequate and experienced supervision.

The report by Mr A. J. Alban of the John Laing Construction Company appears to have been somewhat pessimistic. He thought that the further cost of completing necessary restoration work to put the canal in first-class order was some £10,000–£12,000, which did not include the work needed on the cottages or the provision of plant and improvements. These could amount to a further £30,000 at contractors' prices or £5,000 on a 'make-do' basis with unpaid labour. He estimated that the annual cost of maintenance of the navigation was likely to be in the region of £9,000–£13,000, including the necessary use of four full-time lengthsmen and prison labour. He also considered that the canal could never pay its way and that an annual deficit of at least £4,000–£5,000 was to be expected.

To ensure that the canal was always navigable he considered it essential either to provide a culvert to supply additional water, or to provide two new reservoirs (to be constructed on canal land). While he thought that it was most desirable to have a full-time foreman he conceded that a full-time outside general manager might take the place of the foreman and that it might be possible to appoint such a general manager for the canal who would also be responsible for overseeing the Trust's Packwood House, provided that this latter job took only a very small part of his time.

Although it is not certain how much work remained to be done on the canal after the reopening, there is no doubt that the job was not 100 per cent finished. This statement casts no aspersions on David Hutchings, for he himself, writing in 1981, said:

When the canal was restored . . . [here follows a list of work done] . . . the prime aim was to get the waterway open, working and earning as quickly as possible. It was envisaged that subsequent energetic maintenance and improvement would ensure its full and proper development and eventual prosperity.

From a synthesis of the two reports, the National Trust reached the opinion that:

1   A good deal of work still needs to be done to this canal and thereafter it will need steadily supervised maintenance involving both paid staff and the use of prison labour (volunteers are little help).
2   The canal is unlikely to pay its way but the widely varying estimates of annual deficit can be reduced if capital is spent.
3   In addition, money will have to be spent on equipment and cottages.

By the latter part of 1964 the Trust had concluded that the choice lay between four courses of action:

1   Give notice of termination of the lease.
2   Exercise the option to have the canal permanently vested in the Trust (not necessarily inalienably).
3   Exercise this option to hold the canal, but immediately lease it back to the British Waterways Board for them to manage, or to an organisation or commercial company, the Trust retaining overall control.
4   Ask for the present lease to be extended on the same terms to find out actual costs of maintenance and give time to raise more money.

The Trust apparently had difficulty in reaching a decision since it negotiated a two-month extension to the nominal notice date of 25 March.

At this stage of the account it is pertinent to note that as a result of a political decision to break up completely the British Transport Commission, a new, independent British Waterways Board had, in 1963, taken over the running of all the nationalised inland waterways. At the time of the take-over these were still grouped in three classes, with the future of classes B and C very uncertain (see Chapter 3) and the abandonment of some canals thought unlikely to be commercially useful was still proceeding. Although canals were by now becoming more popular for pleasure cruising, private investment in them was being held back by the doubts about their long-term future. The new board decided that the uncertainties had to be resolved, that no more closures should take place, and that the antagonism which had previously existed between the BTC and the enthusiasts of the IWA had to be replaced by a feeling of partnership.

For a full account of the board's early activities in these directions the reader is referred to *British Canals* by Charles Hadfield, but the main point of relevance to the National Trust's debate about the lease of the southern Stratford is summarised by the following extracts taken from Hadfield:

The Board therefore planned in terms of creating a single cruising network which could be given statutory authority, and so long-term stability . . . The network the Board planned in its first year, explained . . . in *The Future of the Waterways* (1964), backed with detailed figures in *The Facts about the Waterways* (1965) did indeed convince both public and government. The Board's general line was accepted in principle in the White Paper on Transport Policy of July 1966: this, however, had certain objectionable aspects . . . in 1967 a much more acceptable White Paper . . . was issued, a prelude to the 1968 Transport Act which established a cruiseway system little different from the Board's earlier planned network.

Thus, at the time when the National Trust was considering whether to renew its lease of the southern Stratford Canal, the BWB had already published in January 1964, in *The Future of the Waterways*, its preliminary ideas upon a cruiseway network. Mr Hadfield, a member of the BWB from 1963 to 1966, told the author that the Board made considerable efforts to persuade the National Trust to let the lease revert to the BWB. If this had been done, it seems inconceivable that a navigable canal recently restored with so much publicity would not have been included as a cruiseway in the Transport Act of 1968. Indeed, it was then in very reasonable order compared with some others that were so included.

Now, while there is a viewpoint to the effect that the present cruiseway system still leaves a good deal to be desired, and while there is no doubt that the BWB has been consistently starved of money to run it, there is no doubt that at the time of writing (1982) the BWB cruiseway canals are in better order than is the southern Stratford, as will emerge in the subsequent chapter.

However, in 1965 many, if not the majority of the enthusiasts in the IWA were not convinced that the British Waterways Board was any more sincere in its regard for the narrow canals than its predecessor the BTC. Furthermore, the BWB could only propose; the government disposed, and government policies are notoriously liable to change. The National Trust was presumably much influenced by these views and on 28 May 1965 issued a press release of which the salient part is reproduced below.

The National Trust is taking over the freehold of the southern section of the Stratford-upon-Avon Canal next September.

The Trust's decision to take over the canal permanently was made in view of its obligations to its many members, donors, subscribers and volunteers and in the knowledge that it can continue to receive help and advice from the British Waterways Board in this pioneering project. Work remains to be done and an annual deficit of some £6,000 will have to be met, for which funds are now asked. In addition, many improvements, essential for increasing public enjoyment, including a reservoir to hold ten days' supply of water, and moorings have to be provided.

The National Trust welcomes the formation of a separate Trust to make the Upper Avon navigable . . . in order that the canal will cease to be a cul-de-sac.

The wording of this statement suggests that the Trust was very reluctant to take the step, but eventually decided that it had a moral obligation to do so.

During the period between the reopening of the canal and the issuing of the above statement, overall management of the canal had become the responsibility of Sir Dawson Bates, the Trust's area agent at Tewkesbury, and the office side of management was taken over by the then curator of the Trust's nearby property of Packwood House. Mr Hutchings stayed on, in charge of work still proceeding, but became part-time after a while.

It became clear to the Restoration Committee that, although they were still nominally the local agents for the Trust, their influence was now virtually nil. They sought clarification of the situation from the Trust, but heard nothing until February 1965, when an informal letter was received from the Trust's Regional Secretary, Mr Carew Wallace. Formal termination of their responsibility for the canal did not come from the Trust's Head Office until January 1966. The arrangement involving joint membership of the Trust and the Canal Society was, however, left in being and only finally terminated by the Trust in 1973.

Although the committee of the Canal Society had come to expect the termination of its responsibility, its members were naturally aggrieved that they no longer had any formal connection with the canal they had helped to save, and for which they considered that they could still provide useful advice. However, the Stratford-on-Avon Canal Society was reorganised as a sort of 'supporters club' which also represented canal users, as opposed to its previous role which had been almost entirely as a campaign and management body. It offered its co-operation to the Trust in the raising of funds and the provision of work parties. Privately, the committee also noted that it was no longer an agent of the Trust; it was now free to criticise publicly Trust policy should it feel it to be in the best interests of the canal to do so.

Having made its decision on taking the freehold of the canal, the Trust now had to plan a long-term strategy and one of the first priorities was to appoint a new manager. The vacancy was announced as follows:

Now that Mr Hutchings is instructing at the Birmingham College of Architecture, and has agreed to take charge of the restoration of the Upper Avon, a new full-time manager will be appointed by the National Trust. The successful candidate will be required to live in Packwood House, in free quarters, and will also be responsible for paying the staff and giving general supervision there.

Major C. B. Grundy, MC, was appointed early in 1966 and took over in April of that year. After twenty-two years in the army, including service in Korea, he was retiring as Chief Instructor on mortars at a school of infantry. His waterway connections had started early: in *Landscape with Canals* L. T. C. Rolt mentions meeting the Grundy family, with their sons Christopher and Martin, in their boat *Heron* at Nantwich in 1947. Christopher, now Major, Grundy had been a member of the IWA from its formation in 1946 and this was followed by committee membership of and officership in IWA regional branches and then membership of the IWA National Council. He was also a member of both the Lower and Upper Avon Trusts and had worked on the Stratford Canal as a volunteer.

16

Full Circle

During 1964 and 1965 a steady trickle of boats used the canal, but it was only a trickle. An idea of numbers can be gained from the fact that over the Easter period in 1965 something over forty boats were reported to have been down it. Indeed, the National Trust informed the Canal Society in April 1965 that it 'did not think it wise to encourage extensive use of the canal at the moment'. This was primarily because of shortage of water until a new supply system had been arranged with the BWB but also because the Trust were aware of deficiencies in the canal.

Several complaints about the state of the canal were received by the Trust, the Canal Society and the Midlands Branch of the IWA. The trip-boat *Linda*, which has been based at Wootton Wawen, was removed by its owner to Cosgrove on the Grand Union Canal because the physical state of the southern Stratford sometimes prevented fulfilment of contracts. On the other hand, Mr Clover reported at the September 1965 meeting of the Canal Society Committee that he did not experience much trouble in navigating the canal in spite of the considerable draught of his boat, which by then was the ex-tug *Sharpness*.

In fact, the condition of the southern Stratford at that time was probably no worse than that of many canals at the same period, but because the Stratford had been 'restored' many expected it to be in near-perfect condition. It is perhaps unfortunate that the word was ever used. *The Oxford Dictionary* defines it, in this context, as 'To bring back to the original state; to improve repair or retouch (a thing) so as to bring it back to its original condition'. This had not been fully done to the Stratford Canal: more correctly, it had been 'reopened to navigation' with the minimum expenditure of money and time necessary to achieve that objective. It must be remembered that the Stratford was the first canal ever to be reopened by largely voluntary effort and the main objective had been to show that such a thing could be done at all. Later projects on other canals, building on the experience gained on the Stratford, were able to place more emphasis on showing how *well* it could be done.

The circulation of a good deal of unfavourable comment among boaters must have contributed to the relatively slow build-up of usage. In 1966, about 300 boats used the canal which, over a main season of about six months, amounts to an average of less than two per day. However, it must be pointed out that there were far fewer boats on the whole canal system than there are today: the boom in canal boating did not build up until the 1970s.

The amounts of the annual working deficits for the years immediately following reopening are not known because the National Trust never made financial statements available, even when requested to do so. There is no doubt, however, that deficits occurred and by 1970 the Trust was sufficiently concerned to commission a further survey by Messrs Laing. It appears from the report that maintenance was barely keeping up with current deterioration, and that little progress was being made to finalise the repairs that remained after the reopening. Despite the considerable efforts of voluntary work parties, notably those organised by the IWA, this work was still outstanding. The report was critical of this lack of progress and of some aspects of Trust management policy. In that same year overtures were made by the Trust to the BWB concerning the possibility of handing back the canal to them.

Even in 1970 there were still so few boats using the southern section of the Stratford Canal outside holiday periods and weekends that on an ordinary weekday one was liable to find locks being used as 'wet docks' for boats while the owners worked on them. This in itself hardly encouraged greater use since such persons as used the locks in this way did not always vacate them with good grace. However, a steady upward drift began in the volume of boat traffic on all canals, including the Stratford. This was due to an increase of public interest in the amenity value of canals which developed throughout the 1970s and which led to increasing numbers of all types of boats, but of hire craft in particular. By 1972 the boat tolls taken on the southern Stratford amounted to £2,185 which, at £1.50 for boats under 50ft (15.2m) and £2 for those above, as it was at the time, indicates around 1,200–1,300 boats—a four-fold increase over 1966. In spite of this increased income, the estimated deficits for 1972 and 1973 were £8,972 and £11,940 respectively. The 1974 reopening to navigation of the Upper River Avon, from Evesham to a junction with the canal at Stratford, made the southern Stratford Canal part of a through route—an integral part of the 'Avon Ring'. From then on, the canal became in great demand, particularly as there were now not only two hire fleets on the canal itself but also many others on nearby canals and on the Avon. The heavy use which the canal now received was almost certainly greater than even in its commercial heyday; furthermore, this pressure of usage fell on a canal which had still not been brought up to a first-class condition. The very success of the canal in attracting boats now became a problem because, while it brought increased income, it also caused disproportionately increased expenditure resulting from more rapid wear and tear.

The warning sounded by David Hutchings in his 1964 report proved to be all too well-founded as hire boats in the hands of inexperienced or uncaring users battered the banks and gates, literally to fragmentation in some cases. Not all hirers, of course, were inexperienced, or treated the canal irresponsibly; and conversely, not all irresponsible treatment came from hirers. The fact remains, however, that because hirers often are inexperienced, and because the number of hire boats had increased enormously, the canal suffered more damage.

The situation existing by the autumn of 1974 is, perhaps, best illustrated by a quotation from an article of the time by 'Windlass', a contributor to the *Newsletter* of the Stratford-*upon*-Avon Canal Society (as it had by then become). He lived in a lock cottage by the canal.

Along with a good team I was helping to bring a pair of 70-footers from the river at Stratford to the basin at Wootton Wawen. This is a journey involving some 7 or so miles [11km] of canal and 17 locks . . . We left Stratford at 10am in the morning and eventually arrived at Wootton, after a non-stop effort, at 2am the next morning . . . We were faced at each and every lock with a major problem.

Windlass then went on to cite shortage of water, gates that would either not close or not open, and a gate with a metal bracket hanging loose. He said that at the time of writing

. . . the canal has been closed for several weeks due to trouble with the top gate of Lock 26. This year we have had major stoppages as the accepted norm. We have had incidents such as the hire boat which was hung dangerously at 45 degrees on the top sill . . . caused primarily by a run-down set of locks. Lock 36 and Lock 38 each have a paddle 'staunched off'. This means that a broken paddle is put out of use by having its aperture blanked off by a fixed cover, wedged in position. Should either of the single remaining top paddles [at these locks] fail then another total stoppage is inevitable . . . Each year for a long time the general situation has been deteriorating. Gradually work to improve the canal has given way to repairs to maintain it. These in turn have now given way to desperate stop-gap measures simply to try to keep it open. I can only see the situation getting worse as the need for maintenance has given way to an urgent and desperate need for full and total restoration.

The same newsletter also carried a reply to the above article, from Major Grundy, the Canal Manager.

There are some facts which should be corrected. The canal was closed for less than a fortnight owing to the collapse of a gate at Lock 26, and not 'for several weeks'. The statement that 'this year we have had major stoppages as the accepted norm' is quite unfounded. Admittedly there have been minor delays and difficulties from time to time and there was one major stoppage of up to 36 hours when a boat navigating by night drained a three-quarter mile [1.2km] pound. The occasion when a boat sank in a lock with its bow resting on the top sill was entirely due to the inexperience of the crew. It is correct that during the latter part of the season we had to blank off a number of paddles rather than repair them immediately. At that stage paddles were being broken at such a rate that there was no alternative if the canal was to be kept navigable.

Major Grundy went on to point out that problems with paddles would have been far worse had not the Trust embarked, several years previously, on a rolling programme of replacing and resecuring paddles, paddle guides, sills and mechanisms. The resecuring was necessary because

David Hutchings would be the first to admit that a number of methods were adopted at the time of the restoration which were not intended to be permanent. For example, many bottom paddle guides were attached to gates by coach screws rather than by through bolting; top paddle guides were fixed by dogs driven into the masonry and by wooden struts rather than by new bolts secured in new concrete; and gate sills and liners were nailed on with ordinary ungalvanised wire nails rather than with galvanised nails or screws. At the time, these and other similar practices were acceptable but they could not be expected to last and they have not . . . The short life of the top gate at Lock 26 is a cause of great concern as has been the need to replace the balance beams at Locks 25 and 27, all items installed a mere 13 years ago.

(There may be an error here in that records indicate that the top gate of Lock 26 was *not* replaced during restoration.) He then noted that although there had been 3,100 boat-passages of the canal in 1974, the increased traffic had not reduced the financial deficit because it had increased the cost of maintenance. Inflation had also increased costs, but tolls were still the same as in 1972 because they had to bear some relationship to those charged by BWB. Thus, the maintenance cost for 1974 was £15,000 and the deficit £9,000. For comparison, however, the then current cost for maintaining an average 13 miles (21km) of the BWB cruiseway was £38,000: and the southern Stratford has more than three times the national average of locks per mile (1.6km), they being among the most expensive items to maintain.

Major Grundy stated:

It has always been the aim of the Trust, both as an example and a necessity, to maintain and operate the canal with the utmost economy. Not surprisingly, the National Trust is not particularly keen to increase its subsidy to the canal and I, for my part, continue to believe that I should do all that I can to keep expenditure to the irreducible minimum consistent with the canal remaining navigable without undue difficulty.

The article by Windlass must be balanced against the above reply and it is possible that Windlass somewhat overstated the case. Even so, the reply itself indicated that all was not well.

In 1975 the toll was increased to £5 for 14 days for a boat of any length and there was a further increase, to 3,750, in the number of boat passages. From then onwards the pressure of traffic was such that virtually no real maintenance was possible during the summer months. The few permanent staff had to spend an ever-increasing amount of time making emergency repairs just to keep the canal open. However, the Trust tried to improve matters with winter work by both its own staff and at times contractors, and with considerable help from volunteers. Notable among these latter were the numerous work parties under the auspices of the Waterway Recovery Group (formed in 1970 by members of the IWA) and those of the Stratford-upon-Avon Canal Society which by now had a small but dedicated band of workers. These voluntary parties effected several major items of structural work.

The attempt to catch up with some of the backlog of maintenance increased costs still further. In 1976 the toll was raised to £6.50 for one week but income did not rise proportionately in that year because the southern Stratford, in common with many other canals, had to be closed for much of the summer as a result of drought. Thus, total traffic for that year fell to about 2,500 passages, income was about £16,000 and expenditure £26,000. During 1976 it became rumoured that the National Trust proposed to offer the southern Stratford to the Severn-Trent Regional Water Authority. Such a transfer would have been in line with the recommendations of a government Green Paper of 1971, which had proposed the abolition of the British Waterways Board and the transfer of its navigations to water authorities. However, these proposals had been dropped after strong opposition by the canal enthusiasts' lobby.

Early in 1977 rumour crystallised into a statement by the National Trust that 'the Trust would be prepared to transfer the canal to a suitable authority if the opportunity arose, subject to adequate safeguards for the canal's future'. In a letter to *Waterways World* accompanying this announcement, Major Grundy wrote:

In arriving at this conclusion the Trust has taken into account that its original decision to take over the canal . . . was an unusual venture for the National Trust. Because the canal was financially a risky undertaking the Trust, when it accepted the freehold, did not undertake to remain the owner of the Canal for all time and did not declare it inalienable, as is almost invariably the case with properties which the Trust accepts for preservation. The Trust now believes that its pioneer work on the Stratford Canal has been completed and would therefore be willing to transfer it to a suitable authority in the knowledge that the resources of such an authority would be sufficient to enable it to improve the standards of maintenance beyond what has been possible for the National Trust.

There were, however, no takers.

The volume of traffic continued to increase, to 4,100

passages in 1977 and 5,100 in 1978 when the toll was raised to £8. In another letter to *Waterways World*, Major Grundy stated the financial position for 1979: £52,000 had been spent on maintenance; income was £27,000; after receipt of a grant of £5,000 from the Severn-Trent Water Authority and £1,700 from Job Creation funds, this left £18,000 to be found from the general funds of the National Trust.

Because of the unavailability of formal financial accounts it is not possible to equate accurately passages and income. Some boats travel down the canal and back, which presumably counts as two passages but provides only one toll, while others make only a one-way passage. There is also income additional to that from tolls, for example, from residential boats and hire bases. Nevertheless, the income stated for 1979 is somewhat puzzling, since at an increased toll of £9 it seems to indicate a considerable decrease in usage in that year, which is contrary to impressions from personal observation. Unfortunately, no figure for passages was given.

During 1980 it was rumoured that the National Trust was not planning to keep the southern Stratford open beyond the autumn of 1981. In reply to a query from the Canal Society, Mr J. O. Gaze, the Chief Agent of the Trust, stated that the Trust had not decided to close the canal. On the contrary, it was 'trying very hard indeed to find ways and means, not only of keeping it open, but to contrive its maintenance to a higher standard'. However, Mr Gaze further stated that because of its concern about the deficit on running the canal, the Trust was engaged in 'urgent discussions' with the Department of the Environment and expected to have a definite answer from that body by the end of 1980.

The expected answer did not materialise. In a parliamentary reshuffle in January 1981 Mr Marcus Fox, the Parliamentary Under-Secretary of State to the Department of the Environment who had been dealing with the matter, was replaced by Mr Giles Shaw who knew nothing of it. It thus became obvious that no decision was imminent.

An obvious possibility was transfer to the British Waterways Board and when, late in 1980, a party of BWB engineers were seen on an inspection cruise of the canal it became clear that this was under active consideration. The committee of the Stratford Canal Society considered that in the apparent absence of any viable alternative, transfer to the BWB would at least provide long-term security for the canal. They indicated, to both the BWB and the DoE, support for such a transfer provided that the canal received 'cruiseway' status, without which there would be no security. Such was the state of the canal that the BWB would give no assurance on this.

Others, including some members of the Canal Society, regarded transfer to the BWB as a betrayal of everything that had been fought for in saving and restoring the canal. Thus, an *ad hoc* 'Stratford Canal Advisory Committee' (SCAC), centred upon David Hutchings who was still with the Upper Avon Trust, was formed by local members of the IWA and backed in principle by that body. It produced a plan to show how the canal could be renovated and run by a new local trust along the lines of the Upper and Lower Avon Trusts, which were successfully running those navigations.

A meeting of all interested parties, including local authorities, was convened at Packwood House in June 1981 by the DoE. The discussion paper prepared by them for the meeting carried two important statements:

Everyone agrees that the canal should be kept navigable. BWB accept that, if all else fails including their own initiatives, they should take it into their network as a remainder waterway. Closure under Section 112 of the Transport Act 1968 is not considered to be an available option.

The Severn-Trent Water Authority are not prepared to take the responsibility under Section 82 of the Water Resources Act 1963.

At the meeting the National Trust representative stressed that the Trust was not prepared to retain the canal even if sufficient funds could be made available to it; but it was prepared to contribute to a successor with an amount equalling several years' net expenditure. (Current figures for income and gross expenditure were £30,000 and £90,000 respectively.) Although it was not stated at the meeting, there were those who thought it desirable that the National Trust should not retain the canal, since those persons believed that the Trust's management was contributory to the problem.

There was broad agreement between the various parties represented as to the repairs and maintenance required and the word 'restoration' was freely used. However, opinions on method and cost differed widely. The BWB estimated a total of nearly £4 million to cover maintenance arrears alone, to bring the canal up to the highest possible standards over a period of ten years. The SCAC considered that costs could be covered by obtaining initial capital of £½ million which would be invested to cover restoration over three years. It was hoped that the National Trust would provide half this sum and the Severn-Trent Water Authority and the Countryside Commission the balance.

It was noted that the Manpower Services Commission's Special Programme for the unemployed might provide a labour force of up to 68 persons over 3 years to assist with restoration. After completion, the BWB envisaged a requirement for 15 permanent staff, the National Trust considered that 8 would be necessary and the SCAC thought 4, if carefully selected and backed up by volunteers.

The SCAC estimated a potential annual income of £100,000, based on a one-third increase in traffic and two additional hire bases. This, it believed, would be sufficient to cover routine expenditure on maintenance provided that responsibility for road bridges, drainage culverts and hedging could be transferred to other bodies. The BWB assumed no increase in usage as water supply was limiting and estimated an income of £58,000, the increase being based on extra money from existing bases. This amount was not expected to cover routine expenditure.

Three options for future management were discussed, involving the National Trust transferring a freehold or leasehold interest to:

1 A single charitable trust such as the Upper Avon Navigation Trust. This was favoured by the SCAC, but while the NT did not object in principle it found the SCAC's specific proposals unacceptable. In particular, their estimate of income was thought to be overstated and costs understated. Also, the NT would prefer not to enter into leasing arrangements as it was anxious to relieve itself of the canal in a relatively short time.

2 A specially formed consortium, which might include the BWB. Both the BWB and the NT were prepared to consider this but the SCAC were not interested. They sought specific responsibility for the canal.

3 In trust to the BWB to manage to cruising standards with suitable support from local authorities and voluntary organisations. As the BWB were already short of money to fulfil their existing commitments, however, they would need additional finance. Furthermore, the Severn-Trent Water Authority were unlikely to continue the grants which had been made to the canal, if the BWB took over. It was pointed out that realistic guarantees about maintaining the canal to cruiseway standards had yet to be provided by the BWB. There were also fears that voluntary bodies might be reluctant to contribute funds if they had no say in how the money was spent and no opportunity to undertake their own work. (These fears stemmed from the situation prevailing on the Kennet & Avon Canal.)

Discussion eventually polarised around the two extremes contained in the first and third options and the chairman saw no immediate solution likely to meet with general approval. He proposed to report back to Mr Shaw, the Parliamentary Under Secretary of State, on possible lines of action.

In January 1982 the National Trust informed the groups

which had been represented at the Packwood meeting of its conclusion that 'the best solution to the problem of the future of the canal lies in placing it in the care of the British Waterways Board'. Because of the board's lack of money this could not be achieved in a single stage but the BWB had

... indicated that they would be prepared to act as the Trust's agents in the management of the canal for a period of three years, provided that they can be assured of enough money to discharge their duties adequately. They will make no charge for the cost of management. At the end of that period the position would be reviewed and could they then from their own resources afford to assume full responsibility it is hoped they would then do so.

The Trust would make available to the BWB the full revenues of the canal and also a sum each year equivalent to the Trust's deficit over the recent years, up to a maximum over a full three years of £300,000. This would still leave a gap in what was needed, which could not be less than £30,000 per annum if deterioration were checked and might be as much again if it was reversed. The Trust proposed to set up an Advisory Committee formed from the interested organisations to advise the Trust, and through it the BWB, on the running of the canal, and to provide and raise money. To this end, another meeting was to be held at Packwood House in February.

The letter, which was from the Trust's Chief Agent, Mr J. O. Gaze, ended:

I cannot, however, close without telling you plainly that if this solution is not achieved the National Trust will have no recourse other than to apply to the minister for his consent to closure. In making such an application, the National Trust would ask the Minister to recognise that the inability of the DoE to help must be accepted as a major factor.

The possibility of take-over by a local trust, as proposed by the Stratford Canal Advisory Committee, had apparently been rejected entirely.

It was also announced that Major Grundy was resigning as Canal Manager from early in 1982 and that the canal would be temporarily managed on a part-time basis by Mr L. P. Wall, who had recently retired as Area Engineer for the BWB at Birmingham.

In the meantime, the Stratford Canal Advisory Committee had been re-formed into the Stratford Canal Trust with the following objectives:

> . . . to collect sums of money and to take such other steps as may be considered necessary or desirable for preventing the closure to use by the public of the southern Stratford Canal; by acquiring ownership of the canal including its undertaking and assets or by any other means, and of preserving or assisting the preservation of the canal for the use and benefit of the public.

Their main contention was that if only very limited money was to be available for spending on the navigation, they could achieve more with it than could the BWB.

By the next meeting, in February 1982, the situation had changed completely, presumably because of unreported negotiations 'behind the scenes'. The Chairman, Mr Stead of the DoE, first informed the meeting that although the DoE wished the canal to continue as a navigation there would be no money forthcoming from the government and that any planning must not be based on the hope of a future government subsidy. He pointed out that it had not been easy to arrange the increase which had recently been provided in the grant to the BWB to help it with arrears of maintenance on the canals already under its control and that the DoE could not further increase this grant to enable the BWB to take over another waterway. If an application for closure was eventually made, it would be considered objectively at the time and the outcome must not be presumed. The implication was clear. The National Trust's proposals published in January had relied on the hope that at or before the end of the three-year 'reprieve' which it planned, the BWB would be provided with sufficient finance to enable it to take the southern Stratford Canal into its network. Mr Stead was now warning that this was probably a false hope.

Mr Clover and Mr Grazebrook, the representatives of the Stratford Canal Trust, stressed that the SCT offered an alternative. Mr Gaze, for the National Trust, said that now the scheme involving the BWB had fallen through he was prepared to recommend to the Trust that negotiations should be opened with the Stratford Canal Trust, the DoE and the BWB with the objective of passing management responsibilities, but probably not ownership, to the Stratford Canal Trust, by January 1983 if possible.

The general idea was that the freehold of the canal should be transferred to the BWB who would than make it available on a long lease (possibly ninety-nine years) to the SCT at a peppercorn rent. The SCT would hope to negotiate an agreement with the Upper Avon Trust which would allow David Hutchings to take charge of the re-restoration on a part-time basis. Volunteer labour would be used extensively together with any available assistance from the Manpower Services Commission. Before this could take place, the National Trust would need to be satisfied that the SCT was properly constituted and fully representative of all interested parties; that its funding was adequate; and that its proposed programme of work would ensure the safety of the navigation. If, after leasing to the Stratford Canal Trust, that Trust should fail in its obligations, the canal would revert to the BWB as freeholder, with 'remainder' status (that is, not part of the 'cruiseway' network). Any residual liabilities would then fall upon the BWB and not upon the National Trust, who wanted all its liabilities to end with the provision of the £300,000 over the following three years.

Although the BWB was not, at that time, legally empowered to assume freehold ownership, a clause in the 1982 Transport Act, if passed, would enable it to do so. It would, however, still need to be assured of some indemnity from the DoE to cover the problem of residual financial liability (for example, claims arising from a disaster or the cost of works involved in closing the canal).

Thus, less than twenty years after the expenditure of considerable money and toil on the restoration of the southern section of the Stratford-upon-Avon Canal, a new body was about to embark on what was virtually a re-restoration to save the canal from closure. No one wanted to close it now, but there was some doubt as to whether it could be made to pay its way and no one could be sure of obtaining sufficient money to ensure that it stayed open.

It was no longer just the 13 miles (21km) of the southern Stratford Canal that were at stake. The Avon Ring, which had been restored by private enterprise and voluntary effort over a period of thirty years, would be broken if the southern Stratford closed. The entire waterway restoration movement would receive a heavy blow to both its morale and credibility. This book has attempted to show how the Stratford Canal restoration, as the first major canal restoration ever launched, was constrained by special factors which may account for some of the subsequent problems. These factors are not widely known or necessarily acceptable as sufficient reason for the problems and if the canal now has to be permanently closed the majority public reaction may well be that voluntary canal restoration by private enterprise does not and cannot work in the long run.

Is this to be the conclusion which history will record? If it is not to be so, a way must be found to ensure the long-term future of the southern section of the Stratford-upon-Avon Canal. Can the Stratford Canal Trust succeed where the National Trust has conceded? Once again the rallying cry is 'SAVE THE STRATFORD CANAL!'

Postscript

During 1982 the National Trust increased its offer of financial support from £300,000 to £500,000, payable in three instalments over three years. This still fell considerably short of the amount that the Stratford Canal Trust considered necessary. The SCT's considerations were: that payment by instalments would give no opportunity of earning investment income; that the original estimates now needed upward adjustment to allow for inflation; and that it had not proved possible to transfer responsibility for bridges and culverts to public bodies. However, negotiations foundered on a different matter—the specific condition made by the SCT that it required the NT to withdraw its opposition to proposals for the extension of the River Avon Navigation from Stratford to Warwick (the 'Higher Avon Navigation'). The SCT felt that the Higher Avon was vital to the welfare of the canal in that it would remove from it some of the pressure of boat traffic.

Upstream of Stratford the river passes through the National Trust property of Charlecote Park and the NT believed that unacceptable problems would be created by the construction of a necessary lock in the park and uncontrollable public access. It publicly opposed the proposals for a Higher Avon Navigation—as did several influential local organisations and the local authorities— and would not withdraw its opposition in the absence of irrefutable proof that such a navigation had previously existed. The SCT stated that the condition was not negotiable: if it was not accepted the SCT would not undertake the administration of the canal.

In December 1982 the National Trust announced, in a public statement agreed with the SCT, that they could 'go no further with the negotiations'. Thus, as this book goes to press, the fate of the southern section of the Stratford-upon-Avon Canal still hangs in the balance. Will it still be possible to save it, perhaps by arranging some sort of consortium along the lines of option 2 as discussed at the meeting at Packwood House in 1981? Will the canal revert to the British Waterways Board as an unfunded remainder waterway? Or, worst of all, will the National Trust apply for abandonment as they have already mentioned, thus turning the clock back to 1958?

Acknowledgements

I am greatly indebted to the following organisations and persons:

the Stratford-upon-Avon Canal Society for unlimited access to their records; the National Trust for the opportunity to study their records stored at Hughenden; Mr Trevor Cox, District Solicitor of the Stratford-on-Avon District Council, for producing and interpreting legal documents concerning ownership of the Bancroft Gardens and Basin; Mr M. J. Fox for providing invaluable early records and the majority of the photographs; Mr Charles Hadfield for advice and information generously given, and for permission to quote from his published work; Mr John Gagg for permission to use a quotation as a preface; friends in the Stratford-upon-Avon Canal Society for information and comment; and not least my wife, for her help, encouragement and tolerance during the five years of spare-time effort involved in the production of this account.

Index

Figures in italics are plate numbers

Access, 70, 79, 89–92, 115, 127
Agnew, Cmdr Sir Peter, 32
Aickman, Robert, 11, 27, 32, 33
Alban, A. J., 143
Aqueducts, 84, 134, 139, 140; Bearley, 11, 35, 59, 122, 139; Wootton Wawen, 34, 122, 139; Yarningale, 79–80
Armed Services, 131; RAF, 78–9, 87; R. Engineers, 61, 70, 71, 82, 87–9, 94, 111–13, 115–16, 133; R. Pioneers, 115; Territorial, 42, 80; USA, 88
Arnold, Malcolm (composer), 133
Authorising Act (1793), 10, 92, 120
Avon: Ring, 163; River, 84, 111–13, 131–3, 147, 151, 164

Bancroft Basin, 9, 33, 47, 52, 92, 96–114, 116, *5, 9, 12, 14*
Barwell, Douglas, 32
Bates, Sir Dawson, 48, 128, 147
Benn, H. E. M., 135
Bentonite, 59, 60
Beran, Mr, 59
Berry, E., 59, 129
Birmingham Angling Assoc, 61
Birmingham Canal Nav, 116, 118
Birmingham Post, the, 12, 44
Bishopton, 42–3, 52, 118, *2, 7*
Boucher, Dr Cyril, 59, 93
Bowes Cttee, 26–30, 42
Bridges, 134, 139–40; Banbury Rd, 110–12; Canada, 83, 117, 121;

Featherbed Lane, 10, 12–13, 27, 34–5, 43–4, 46, 61, 82–3, 125, *1*; Lifford Lane, 12, 20; Maidenhead Rd, 92; One Elm, 87, 116; Preston Bagot, 34; Bishopton Spa, 117; Timothy's, 61, 119–20; Warwick Rd, 92
Bridges, Lord, 38
Burr, Mr, 109
Burton, Don, 13, 39, 42, 52, 118
Butler, Mr, 53

Cadbury Trust, 135
Calor Ltd, 118
Canal Cruising Co, 19
Cane, Mr, 39
Canoe, 9, 14–15, 16, 35, 44
Carew Wallace, Mr, 147
Chesham, Lord, 75–6
Civic Trust, 76
Clayton, F. G. B., 41, 54, 58–9
Clifford, Christopher, 33, 39, 41, 54
Clover, Stanley, 76, 149, 162
Countryside Commission, 158
Coventry Canal Soc, 32, 35–6
Crawford & Balcarres, The Earl of, 38, 133
Cruiseway, 145–6, 154, 157, 159, 162

Dick's Lane, 60–1, 74, 76, 140, *10, 11*
Donors, 62, 77, 135, 146
Dredging, 58, 134, 138–9; access for, 79, 90–2, 111, 116; in first two years, 60–2, 77, 78–82, *3*; in last year, 87–8, 94, 116, 118; of Bancroft Basin, 111–13, *9*; of locks, 66,

117, 138; technique, 72–5, 78–82, 89–91

Environment, Dep of the, 156–7, 160, 161–2

Feeney, J., Trust, 135
Finance, 38, 48, 80, 110, 113, 137, 160, 162, 164; deficits, 135, 140–1, 143, 144, 146, 150–1, 153–6, 160; donations, 55, 77, 95, 135, 148; estimates, 51, 58–61, 107, 128–30, 143, 158, 160; expenditure, 61, 75, 77, 79, 82, 95, 109, 113, 118, 134–5, 141, 143, 150, 154–6, 158; grants, 52, 95, 135, 156, 158, 159, 161; income, 46, 48, 61–2, 118, 140, 151, 155–6, 158, 159
Flower, Sir Fordham, 9
Fox, Marcus, 159
Fox, Michael J., 4, 13, 14, 15, 27, 38, 63, 80, 109
French, D., 59, 73, 129

Gaze, J. O., 156, 160, 162
Gilbert, C. J., 48, 59, 127
Goodland, E. G., 11
Grand Union Canal, 12, 38, 149
Gray, Gordon, 135
Grazebrook, Nicholas, 162
Grundy, Maj Christopher B., 148, 152–4, 155–6, 161

Hadfield, Charles (author), 23, 26, 35, 145–6
Hancox, O., 48, 52, 59, 61, 127, 128–9
Hind, Lady, Trustees of, 135
Hutchings, R. David E., 4, 33, 41, 53, 55, 59, 105, 108, 109, 122, 147, *8*; and

Upper Avon, 148, 157; appointment as manager, 48, 56; as rally organiser, 123; criticism of, 80, 132, 153; in Coventry Canal Soc, 32; in Protection Cttee, 13; in Stratford Canal Advisory Cttee & Trust, 157, 162; personal qualities, 62, 136; reports by, 60, 62, 73, 76, 80–1, 87–9, 92–5, 115–18, 137–43, 144, 151; residence of, 56, 127

Industrial Design & Construction Ltd, 119
Inland Waterways Ass, 11–13, 27, 32, 33, 35, 40, 55, 145, 146, 148, 157; Bulletin, 13, 14; disagreement within, 39; Festival of Boats & Arts (1964), 9, 106, 117, 121, 123–4, 131–3, *14*; Midlands Branch, 12, 13, 32, 39, 52, 53, 76, 149; National Boat Rally 1957, 32; opposing abandonment, 32, 33; work parties, 76, 115, 142, 150, 154
Inspection Cruise, 75–6, 122–3, *13*

James, William (engineer), 125
Johnson, James, 32
Jones, Miss F., 135

Keer, Mr, 57
Kennet & Avon Canal, 46, 159; Ass, 23, 28
Kerr, Sir Reginald, 25–6, 35, 40, 41
King, Douglas, 104, 123, 135
Knight, Brian, 71, 81, 116, 118, 142, *12*

Laing Construction Co, 111, 113; reports by, 137, 143–4, 150
Lapworth (and Kingswood), 54–5, 56, 60, 76, 78, 125, 137, 140, 141, *3*, *10*, *11*
Latham, R. S., 48
Leaks, 10, 11, 16, 17, 21, 28, 58–9, 121–2, 139, 140

Lease (and Freehold), 41, 55, 130; disposal by NT, 159, 162; initial to NT, 41, 46, 124, 129, 137, 144, 146; long-term to NT, 127, 144, 146; of Bancroft Basin, 97–101; terms of, 105, 107, 110
Llangollen Canal, 20, 26
Local Management (Restoration) Cttee, 61, 80–1, 104, 119–20, 122–4, 128; appointment of, 47–8, 56; relationship with NT, 47–8, 81, 106–10, 119–20, 147–8
Lock, 60–1, 132, 134–5, 138–9, 164; before restoration, 11, 27–8, 57–8, 64; dimensions, 93, 94, 132, 140; gates, 53–4, 57, 60, 64, 66–9, 70–1, 77, 88–9, 116, 117–18, 121, 134–5, 138, 151, 152, *4*, *12*; maintenance, 139–40, 152, 153; repairs in first two years, 61, 62, 71–2, 78, 81, 82, 83–4; repairs in last year, 88–9, 92–4, 115–16, 117–18, 120–1; technique of repair, 64–71, 93–4, *4*, *7*, *8*, *12*
Lock & Quay magazine, 24
Lower Avon Navigation Trust, 24, 26, 28, 32, 148, 157
Lowles, Sir Geoffrey, 76
Lowsonford, 42, 64, 74, 76, 78, 79, 121, 140
Lumley Saville Ltd, 57

Macfarlane, M. J., 133
Maidstone Gaol, 111
Manpower Services Commission, 158, 162
Massey Ferguson Ltd, 57
Montgomeryshire Canal, 70, 116, 118
Morton, Leslie, 33
Mud boards, 73–5, 78, 90–1, *3*
Munk, Capt L. R., 33, 76

National Trust, The, 36, 59, 61, 65, 80–1, 92, 101, 123–4, 133–6, 149, 163; acceptance of Strat. Canal, 38, 40–1, 46–53,

56; and Bancroft Basin, 104–10, 113; and cottages, 125–30; and Timothy's Bridge, 119–20; considering canals, 33, 38; disposal of Strat. Canal, 155–62, 164; long-term lease to, 137, 144–8; policy on maintenance, 150, 153, 154
New Basin, 97, 98, 104, 107, 112
New Cut, 104–8

Oxford Canal, 40; Assoc, 23

Packwood House, 141, 143, 147, 148; meetings at, 157–60, 161–2, 164
Pilgrim Trust, 55, 135
Pinder, J., 15, 56
Preston Bagot, 34, 35, 41, 43, 75, 78, 118, 140
Prisoners, 88, 89, 94, 95, 111, 113, 115, 118, 121, 141, 142–4
Protection Cttee, 13–14
Protest: cruise, 35; form, 36; meeting, 32–3, 35

Queen Elizabeth the Queen Mother, 124, 133, *14*

Railway & Canal Traffic Act (1888), 14, 31, 36, 44
Railway Companies, 23; British Railways, 51; Great Western, 10, 64, 97–101; Oxford, Worcester & Wolverhampton, 97; West Midland, 97
Rathbone, E., 135
Rathbone, J. F. W., 48, 75, 105, 109
Right of Navigation, 10, 14, 29, 31
Rolt, L. T. C. (author), 12, 148
Rover, Co, the, 56

Scott, Francis C., Trust, 135
Severn River Authority (and Severn Trent Water Authority), 112, 155, 156, 157, 158, 159

Shakespeare Theatre, 97, 98–9, 101, 133
Shaw, Giles, 156, 159
Shell-BP, 133
Shropshire Union Canal, 20
Smith, John L. E., 4, 33, 38, 40, 41, 42, 46, 48, 55, 76
Staffing: after reopening, 137–8, 141, 143–4, 154, 158; during restoration, 59, 75
Staffordshire & Worcestershire Canal, 20, 38, 41; Soc, 89
Statistics (restoration), 134–5
Stead, Mr, 161–2
Steam pump, 53, 56
Stratford Canal Advisory Cttee, 157, 158–9, 160, 161
Stratford Canal Club, 12, 13
Stratford Canal, northern, 9, 12, 20, 25, 27, 29
Stratford Canal Trust, 161, 162, 163, 164
Stratford-on-Avon Canal Soc (and 'upon'), 14, 22, 38–40, 46–8, 126, 147–9, 156, 157; canoe trip, 9, 14–15; early proposals by, 16–17, 39; magazine (Cut & Trust), 14, 62–3, 71–3, 76–8; membership, 14, 17, 48, 147; newsletter, 35, 40, 42, 63, 152; opposition to abandonment by, 32–3, 35–7, 44; report to Bowes Cttee, 27–8; work parties, 41–3, 127, 142, 148, 154, 2
Stratford-on-Avon Rural District Council, 14, 99, 101, 110, 127–8, 129
Stratford-upon-Avon Borough Corporation (Council), 13, 14, 31–2, 34, 47, 87, 92, 97–108, 109–11, 113–14, 119–20, 128–9

Stratford-upon-Avon Herald, the, 76, 101, 107, 113
Sunday Times, the, 136

Thames & Severn Canal, 70
Thomas, Mr, 52, 93–4
Toll, 9, 14, 122, 151, 153–6; tickets, 9, 14–15, 36–7, 44
Tompkins, J. D., 119
Tramway: Stratford, 97–9, 100, 105; Wilmcote, 116
Transport Acts: (1947), 23; 1953, 24; (1960), 47; 1968, 29, 145, 157; (1982), 162
Transport (Commission) Waterways, British, 9, 19, 33, 34–5, 53, 101, 122, 127, 145, 146; assistance from, 54, 56, 57–9, 70, 71; Board of Survey (1954), 10, 24–5, 26, 29; discussions with re Strat. Canal, 16–17, 33, 41, 46, 104, 129; formation & policy, 23–6, 29, 58, 69, 127
Transport, Minister & Ministry of, 40, 46, 87, 93, 94, 104, 139; and warrant of abandonment, 31, 36, 39, 43–4; grant, 46, 52, 55, 95, 135
Trent & Mersey Canal, 19
Turriff Construction Co, 57, 81

Upper Avon Navigation Trust, 147, 148, 157, 159, 162

Volunteer labour, 24, 63, 76, 81, 89, 106, 115, 117, 131, 136, 143, 146, 148, 150, 163; early clearance by, 41–3, 52–3; maintenance by, 140–1, 150, 154, 158, 162; proposed use of, 13, 16–17, 51, 58; usefulness of, 141–3, 144; work

by, 64–6, 71, 73, 75, 116, 118, 154

Wall, L. P., 161
Warrant of Abandonment, 9, 31–7, 43–4, 160, 164
Warwick Rural District Council, 129–30
Warwickshire County Council, 9, 13, 31, 34–5, 36–7, 43, 45, 46, 61, 82, 104, 122
Water supply, 10, 28, 46, 58–9, 62, 123, 131, 143, 147, 149, 152, 158
Waterway Recovery Group, 154
Waterways Board, British, 93, 106, 137, 139, 140, 144, 146, 149, 155, 161; formation and cruiseway policy, 145–6, 154; return of canal to, 150, 157, 158–64
Waterways Redevelopment Board, 29, 42, 46, 101
Waterways World magazine, 155–6
Weed boom, 12, 20
Wilmcote, 125, 140
'Windlass' (author), 152, 154
Winson Green Gaol, 88, 89, 94, 95, 111, 113, 115, 118
Winter 1962–3, 84, 5, 6
Wootton Wawen, 11, 34, 78, 81, 122, 125, 132, 140, 149, 152
Work parties, 41–2, 43, 52–3, 61, 72, 148, 150, 154
Wormwood Scrubs Gaol, 113
Wyckham Blackwell Ltd, 53, 70, 110
Wyrley & Essington Canal, 57, 70, 116

Yarningdale, 78, 79